america & russia: from cold war confrontation to coexistence

"LET'S GET A LOCK FOR THIS THING."

america & russia: from cold war confrontation to coexistence

EDITED BY GARY R. HESS

Bowling Green State University

problem studies in american history

Thomas Y. Crowell Company
New York
Established 1834

Library of Congress Cataloging in Publication Data

HESS, GARY R., ed.
    America and Russia: from Cold War confrontation to
coexistence.

    CONTENTS: American policy and the origins of the
Cold War, 1945–53: Bernstein, B. J. The revisionist
critique of American policy. Gaddis, J. L. A defense
of American policy. Feis, H. Containment as a response
to European crises. Gardner, L. C. Dean Acheson and
"situations of strength." Adler, L. K. and Paterson,
T. G. "Red fascism" and the development of the Cold
War. [etc.]

    1. United States—Foreign relations—Russia.
2. Russia—Foreign relations—United States.
3. United States—Foreign relations—1945–
I. Title.
E183.8.R9H47   327.73'047   72-10916
ISBN 0-690-05869-1

*The frontispiece cartoon is from Herbert
Block,* Straight Herblock *(New York:
Simon and Schuster, 1964), p. 77.
Reprinted by permission of Herbert Block.*

TO EDWARD YOUNGER

preface

This collection of essays is intended to provide a
comprehensive understanding of the Cold War. The first
several selections concentrate on the 1945–53 period;
that phase of Russian-American relations is the subject of
much recent historical writing which, as a whole,
underscores the complexity of the early Cold War and
the difficulty of tracing and assigning responsibility. The
essays dealing with the 1953–62 period illustrate the
immense impact of the early Cold War as the movement
toward coexistence repeatedly encountered opposition from
entrenched Cold Warriors in Moscow and Washington.
While historians cannot write definitively of recent
developments, a final article offers one historian's
interpretation on the decline of the Cold War during
the last decade.

In approaching any historical problem, we must not
only become familiar with the basic facts but should also
observe how historians interpret the data. Are the historian's
conclusions reasonable in light of the evidence presented?
Does the historian ignore important facts and developments?
Thus it is hoped that these selections will be read
critically, enabling the reader to develop some well-founded
and thoughtful perspectives on the Cold War.

While preparing this volume, I have benefited from the
valuable advice of my colleagues William Rock and
Bernard Sternsher, the assistance of Mrs. Cheryl Walker
and Mrs. Gayle Morris, and, finally, by the questions and
comments of students in my course on the history of
American foreign policy.

Gary R. Hess

contents

america & russia: from cold war confrontation to coexistence

introduction

The Cold War confrontation between the United States and
the Soviet Union dominated international relations from
1945 until the early 1960s. Much speculation and
controversy has ensued as to who and what were
responsible for the events that brought about the Cold War.
As early as 1946, Walter Lippmann, commenting on the
failure of the Big Three to settle more than a few of the
major issues, wrote that it was "a failure of diplomacy."[1]
Can we justifiably attribute the entire period of the Cold
War to a failure of diplomacy? No scholar has offered a
conclusive answer, but the essays that follow explore facets
of the question.

By 1949 the Cold War, originating in disagreements
and misunderstandings involving post–World War II
European political questions, divided the European
continent into Russian and American spheres of
influence. With the lines drawn in Europe, the two
nations competed for dominance in other parts of the
world—the Middle East, Latin America, Asia, Africa.
An unchecked arms race culminated in the stockpiling of
nuclear weapons and the development of intercontinental
missile systems.

Despite intense and costly struggles and occasional crises,
however, the year 1953 saw the beginning of a substantial,
if gradual and uneven, improvement in American-Russian
relations. After confrontations over Berlin and Cuba in
1961–62, a degree of peaceful coexistence was finally
attained; and the signing of the Nuclear Test Ban Treaty
in 1963 marked, in the words of President Kennedy, "an
important first step—a step toward peace— a step toward
reason—a step away from war."[2] However, while the Cold
War in its classic form may have ended, its legacy—
notably the unresolved differences over several critical
issues—hinders the movement toward a Russian-American
détente.

One approach to considering the Cold War in its
historical perspective lies in examining various phases of
American diplomacy in terms of motivation, objectives, and
influence, from there to evaluate United States policy in
response to the challenges of the Cold War. In formulating

[1] Walter Lippmann, "A Year of Peacemaking," *Atlantic Monthly*
178 (December 1946): 40.
[2] *Department of State Bulletin* 49 (August 12, 1963): 235.

1

its policies toward the Soviet Union, did the United States accurately perceive Soviet interests and actions, or did erroneous assumptions lead to misunderstanding of the other side? Has United States policy tended to be measured and appropriate, or has it, at least on occasion, constituted an overreaction? What effect has United States policy had on the Soviet Union? Has the policy encouraged a reduction or a heightening of tensions?

Part I explores the origin and development of the Cold War from 1945 to 1953. Orthodox American interpretation has attributed the Cold War to the aggressive policies of the Soviet Union. To Americans who can recall World War II and its aftermath, as well as to many scholars, the Soviets abruptly ended the wartime coalition and initiated the Cold War by disregarding agreements reached at Yalta and Potsdam and clamping an "iron curtain" over the countries of Eastern Europe. Many also believed that the Soviets effectively crippled the young United Nations by irresponsibly exercising their veto power in the Security Council, and thus when the Russians began pressuring Greece and Turkey, the United States was forced to respond in 1947 with the policy of containment against further Soviet expansion.

Within the past decade, a group of historians have offered a revisionist interpretation of the causes of the Cold War. The revisionists, a part of the New Left school that has reinterpreted many phases of American history, are representative of the intellectual and political turmoil of the 1960s, during which the Vietnam war, the development of coexistence, and the debate over national priorities have opened to question the assumptions of American foreign policy since World War II. While differing among themselves on many points, the revisionists underscore that both sides were responsible for the Cold War. According to their writings, the United States erred in several ways, causing the Soviets to view American policy with suspicion and even fear. President Harry Truman is regarded as having abruptly abandoned Franklin Roosevelt's efforts at conciliating the Russians, embarking instead upon a policy which, from the Soviet point of view, appeared offensive. Enjoying sole possession of the atomic bomb, and having the largest navy and air force in the world, the United States at the end of World War II dominated the Pacific, Western Europe, and Latin America and sought to extend its influence into Russian-dominated Eastern Europe. American policy included the curtailing of Lend-Lease, refusing to grant a postwar reconstruction loan requested by the Soviets, and, in the opinion of some revisionists, using the atomic bomb as a means of intimidating the Russians. The containment policy, according to this view, was provocative, forcing the Soviets to take countermeasures in order to solidify their position in Eastern Europe.

Barton J. Bernstein presents the revisionist interpretation, a criticism of American policy of 1945–46 beginning with Truman's succession to the presidency. According to Bernstein, an insecure Soviet Union sought modest goals in Eastern Europe only to be repeatedly rebuffed by an aggressive American diplomacy. John Lewis Gaddis, however, disagrees. While acknowledging that the United States failed to understand Soviet objectives after World War II, Gaddis maintains that American leaders by 1946 reasonably perceived a threat to the nation's security and responded accordingly. Sharply criticizing the revisionist position, Gaddis argues that the Soviets, not the Americans, had the greater opportunity to avert the Cold War.

The announcement of the Truman Doctrine, justifying the policy of containment, marked the point at which the issues between America and Russia were fully realized. In requesting congressional support for assistance to Greece and Turkey in 1947, President Truman also called for the assumption of a broad, far-reaching obligation to "help free peoples to maintain their free institutions and their national integrity against aggressive movements that seek to impose upon them totalitarian regimes." The aid to Greece and Turkey was approved, and in the following two years, the structure of the containment policy was completed with massive United States commitment to the economic revival of Western Europe (the Marshall Plan) and the formation of a military alliance linking the United States to the non-Communist nations of Europe (the North Atlantic Treaty Organization).

The Truman Doctrine was a landmark in the Cold War. Scholars have debated many questions raised by the presumptions of American policy. Did the Soviet Union threaten Greece and Turkey? Could assistance to those nations have been provided through the United Nations? Did the Soviets have designs on Western Europe? Did the containment policy force the division of Europe and undermine negotiations on the German and eastern-European questions? Herbert Feis offers the traditional American viewpoint in *From Trust to Terror,* in which containment is presented as a defensive policy necessary to preserve Europe from Soviet domination. Lloyd Gardner, however, in *Architects of Illusion,* questions Soviet aggressiveness and argues that the United States was determined to take the offensive in 1947. Gardner concentrates on the role of Under Secretary of State Dean Acheson, whom he sees as obsessed with building "situations of strength" against the Soviets. In pursuit of the "open door" and emboldened by its success in the Iranian crisis of 1946, the United States, Gardner avers, forced the division of Europe in 1947–48.

Revisionists as well as many traditionalists concur, although in varying degrees, that the United States failed to appreciate the limited objectives of Soviet diplomacy after World War II. In an assessment of American perceptions of the Soviet Union, Les K. Adler and Thomas G. Paterson argue that a blurring of Nazi Germany and Soviet Russia in the American consciousness ("Red Fascism") of the 1940s and 1950s contributed to the public's marked hostility toward the Soviet Union and the consensus behind the containment policy.

Part II examines American policy from 1953 to 1962, an era of transition in the Cold War. The writings on this period are not as extensive, nor have they been as contentious, as those of the early Cold War. While the availability of fewer primary sources and memoirs contributes in part to this development, another major consideration is that the Eisenhower administration stimulated little controversy among contemporaries; this pattern tends to carry into the nature of historical writing. Thus, historians do not display the sharp disagreement on Eisenhower's foreign policy that marks their appraisals of the Truman, Kennedy, and Johnson administrations.

In the excerpt from his history of the Cold War, scholar-diplomat Louis Halle examines the efforts of Stalin's successors to promote coexistence. While acknowledging that an end to the Cold War was not yet possible, Halle criticizes the rigidity and hesitancy of the American response to the Soviet overtures of 1953–55. Indeed, there is a general agreement among writers that American policy under Eisenhower lacked the flexibility necessary to take advantages of changes in the Cold War. Halle accepts the traditional American interpretation of the origins of the Cold War (he was working in the State Department when the containment policy was adopted), but he contends that the changed international situation after Stalin's death warranted modification in the American position.

Adam B. Ulam explores the complex motivations behind Soviet policy of 1958–60 which led both to a crisis over Berlin and, in a seeming paradox, to a search for cooperation with the United States. According to Ulam, Premier Nikita Khrushchev, who had emerged from the post-Stalin power struggle as the dominant figure in the Russian leadership, conducted his foreign policy in the midst of perils that were not fully appreciated by the West. While crediting Eisenhower with some flexibility in pursuing the coexistence objective, Ulam does criticize the United States for insensitivity to the problems plaguing Khrushchev and for ineptitude in handling the U-2 incident.

Pursuing some of the themes raised by Ulam, William G. Carleton explores the response of the Kennedy administration to the more fluid international situation generated by the decline of the bipolar world. Carleton contends that Kennedy failed to initiate desirable changes in foreign policy and instead "needlessly . . . fanned the tensions of the Cold War." It was after the Cuban missile crisis of October 1962 that Kennedy, according to Carleton, substantially modified his position and began to pursue coexistence.

American and Russian actions in the missile crisis, the climactic event of the Cold War, have been widely debated. What was the Soviet motive in installing the missiles in Cuba? Did the United States accurately perceive the Soviet intentions and the military significance of the missiles? Did American policy during the crisis achieve its objectives? Andrew Horelick argues that the Soviet effort sought to achieve a temporary strategic gain in order to offset a nuclear imbalance. Regarding American diplomacy as effective in assessing the Soviet maneuvers and in forcing the Soviets to assume the responsibility of a showdown, Horelick believes that the Soviet promise to withdraw its missiles solidified the American strategic position.

Within a year of the missile crisis, the United States and the Soviet Union took the first steps in the direction of peaceful coexistence. With the signing of the Nuclear Test Ban Treaty in 1963, many observers suggested that the Cold War had virtually ended. In Part III, in an article written in 1969, Brian Thomas discusses the development of Russian-American understanding. Coexistence, defined by one Soviet specialist as meaning "that the superpowers recognized the necessity for averting the catastrophe of mutual nuclear annihilation and groped toward establishing certain urgent but defined limits to their exercise of power,"[3] indeed seemed to characterize the Soviet-American relationship described by

[3] Philip E. Mosely, "The United States and East-West Détente: The Range of Choice," *Journal of International Affairs* 22 (1968): 5–15.

Thomas. Could the two nations now move toward détente—a firmer basis for international stability and the resolution of differences "through balanced, reciprocal, and mutually beneficial concessions"?[4] It may be too early to answer that question fully, but developments of recent years are encouraging. President Nixon, a classic Cold Warrior in the 1940s and 1950s, has repeatedly expressed his hope to move from the era of "confrontation" to the era of "negotiation." The mining of Haiphong Harbor in May 1972 did not, despite predictions to the contrary, result in Soviet cancellation of the Moscow Summit Conference, and the Moscow conference witnessed several important agreements, most notably the treaty limiting strategic arms.

Wars, hot or cold, seldom result from irreconcilable differences between nations. And, in this instance, is it becoming increasingly clearer that the Cold War could have been averted, or at least minimized, had more effective and realistic diplomatic actions been taken by the Americans and the Soviets? From these readings on the origins and development of the Cold War, does the Russian-American confrontation emerge as a series of mutual misunderstandings, of actions based on self-fulfilling prophecies, and of missed opportunities to reconcile differences? Does the movement toward coexistence help to underscore the relative insignificance of many early Cold War issues? For instance, with the policies of the United States during the Hungarian crisis of 1956 and the Czech crisis of 1968 in effect recognizing the Soviet domination of those and other central and eastern European nations, the American concern with Eastern Europe during the 1940s seems quixotic, and certainly not essential to American interests. With these changed perspectives, does the evidence suggest that the responsibility for the Cold War and its prolongation is not to be traced so much to villains as to leaders in Moscow and Washington who failed to be effective statesmen?

4 Ibid.

part one
american policy and the origins of the cold war, 1945–53

one
the revisionist critique of american policy

BARTON J. BERNSTEIN

*One of the principal proponents of the New Left
interpretation of the American past is Barton J. Bernstein,
professor of history at Stanford University. Bernstein,
born in New York City in 1936, received his A.B. from
Queens College and his Ph.D. from Harvard in
1963. He coedited* The Truman Administration: A
Documentary History *(1966), and edited* Towards a New
Past: Dissenting Essays in American History *(1968),
a collection of New Left writings, including two of his
own essays on the shortcomings of liberalism during the
New Deal and World War II.* Politics and Policies of
the Truman Administration *(1970), from which the
following selection is taken, is a compilation of essays
critical of the Truman presidency, with articles by
Bernstein on the origins of the Cold War and Truman's
civil rights program. In his determination to underscore
American hostility toward Russia in 1945–46, does Bernstein
ignore incidents and factors which Americans reasonably
perceived as constituting Russian aggressiveness?*

> *"There is no nation which has
> attitudes so pure that they cannot
> be bettered by self-examination."*
> —John Foster Dulles (1946)

Source: Barton J. Bernstein, "American Foreign Policy and
the Origins of the Cold War," in *Politics and Policies of the
Truman Administration,* ed. Barton J. Bernstein (Chicago:
Quadrangle, 1970), pp. 15–17, 23–40. Copyright © 1970
by Quadrangle Books, Inc. Reprinted by permission of
the publisher.

9

"We are forced to act in the world
as it is, and not in the world as
we wish it were, or as we would
like it to become."
—Henry L. Stimson (1947)

Despite some dissents, most American scholars have reached a general consensus on the origins of the Cold War. As confirmed internationalists who believe that Russia constituted a threat to America and its European allies after World War II, they have endorsed their nation's acceptance of its obligations as a world power in the forties and its desire to establish a world order of peace and prosperity. Convinced that only American efforts prevented the Soviet Union from expanding past Eastern Europe, they have generally praised the containment policies of the Truman Doctrine, the Marshall Plan, and NATO as evidence of America's acceptance of world responsibility. While chiding or condemning those on the right who opposed international involvement (or had even urged preventive war), they have also been deeply critical of those on the left who have believed that the Cold War could have been avoided, or that the United States shared substantial responsibility for the Cold War.

Whether they are devotees of the new realism or open admirers of moralism and legalism in foreign policy, most scholars have agreed that the United States moved slowly and reluctantly, in response to Soviet provocation, away from President Franklin D. Roosevelt's conciliatory policy. The Truman administration, perhaps even belatedly, they suggest, abandoned its efforts to maintain the Grand Alliance and acknowledged that Russia menaced world peace. American leaders, according to this familiar interpretation, slowly cast off the shackles of innocence and moved to courageous and necessary policies.

Despite the widespread acceptance of this interpretation, there has long been substantial evidence (and more recently a body of scholarship) which suggests that American policy was neither so innocent nor so nonideological; that American leaders sought to promote their conceptions of national interest and their values even at the conscious risk of provoking Russia's fears about her security. In 1945 these leaders apparently believed that American power would be adequate for the task of reshaping much of the world according to America's needs and standards.

By overextending policy and power and refusing to accept Soviet interests, American policy-makers contributed to the Cold War. There was little understanding of any need to restrain American political efforts and desires. Though it cannot be proved that the United States could have achieved a *modus vivendi* with the Soviet Union in these years, there is evidence that Russian policies were reasonably cautious and conservative, and that there was at least a basis for accommodation. But this possibility slowly slipped away as President Harry S. Truman reversed Roosevelt's tactics of accommodation. As American demands for democratic governments in Eastern Europe became more vigorous, as the new administration delayed in providing economic assistance to Russia and in seeking international control of atomic energy, policy-makers met with increasing Soviet suspicion and antagonism. Concluding that Soviet-American cooperation was impossible, they came to believe that the Soviet state could be halted only by force or the threat of force.

The emerging revisionist interpretation, then, does not view American actions simply as the necessary response to Soviet challenges, but instead tries to understand American ideology and interests, mutual suspicions and misunderstandings, and to investigate the failures to seek and achieve accommodation.

· · · · ·

Roosevelt's successor was less sympathetic to Russian aspirations and more responsive to those of Roosevelt's advisers, like Admiral William Leahy, Chief of Staff to the Commander in Chief; Harriman; James Forrestal, Secretary of the Navy; and James F. Byrnes, Truman's choice for Secretary of State, who had urged that he resist Soviet efforts in Eastern Europe. As an earlier self-proclaimed foe of Russian communism, Truman mistrusted Russia. ("If we see that Germany is winning the war," advised Senator Truman after the German attack upon Russia in 1941, "we ought to help Russia, and if Russia is winning we ought to help Germany and in that way kill as many as possible.") Upon entering the White House, he did not seek to follow Roosevelt's tactics of adjustment and accommodation. Only eleven days in the presidency and virtually on the eve of the United Nations conference, Truman moved to a showdown with Russia on the issue of Poland.

Poland became the testing ground for American foreign policy, as Truman later said, "a symbol of the future development of our international relations." At Yalta the three powers had agreed that the Soviet-sponsored Lublin Committee (the temporary Polish government) should be "reorganized on a broader democratic basis with the inclusion of democratic leaders from Poland itself and from Poland abroad." The general terms were broad: there was no specific formula for the distribution of power in the reorganized government, and the procedures required consultation and presumably unanimity from the representatives of the three powers. The agreement, remarked Admiral Leahy, was "so elastic that the Russians can stretch it all the way from Yalta to Washington without ever technically breaking it." ("I know, Bill—I know it. But it's the best I can do for Poland at this time," Roosevelt replied.)

For almost two months after Yalta the great powers haggled over Poland. The Lublin Committee objected to the Polish candidates proposed by the United States and Great Britain for consultation because these Poles had criticized the Yalta accord and refused to accept the Soviet annexation of Polish territory (moving the eastern boundary to the Curzon Line). In early April Stalin had offered a compromise—that about 80 per cent of the cabinet posts in the new government should be held by members of the Lublin Committee, and that he would urge the committee to accept the leading Western candidates if they would endorse the Yalta agreement (including the Curzon Line). By proposing a specific distribution of power, Stalin cut to the core of the issue that had disrupted negotiations for nearly three months, and sought to guarantee the victory he probably expected in Poland. Roosevelt died before replying, and it is not clear whether he would have accepted this 4 to 1 representation; but he had acknowledged that he was prepared to place "somewhat more emphasis on the Lublin Poles."

Now Truman was asked to acknowledge Soviet concern about countries on her borders and to assure her influence in many of these countries by granting her friendly (and probably nondemocratic) governments, and even by letting her squelch anti-communist democrats in countries like Poland. To the President and his advisers the issue was (as Truman later expressed Harriman's argument) "the extension of Soviet control over neighboring states by independent action. we were faced with a barbarian invasion of Europe." The fear was not that the Soviets were about to threaten all of Europe but that they had designs on Eastern Europe, and that these designs conflicted with traditional American values of self-determination, democracy, and open markets.

Rushing back to Washington after Roosevelt's death, Harriman found most of FDR's advisers (now Truman's) sympathetic to a tougher approach. At a special White House meeting Harriman outlined what he thought were the Soviet Union's two policies—cooperation with the United States and Great Britain, and the creation of a unilateral security ring through domination of its border states. These policies, he contended, did not seem contradictory to Russian leaders, for "certain elements around Stalin" misinterpreted America's generosity and desire to cooperate as an indication of softness and concluded "that the Soviet Government could do anything that it wished without having any trouble with the United States." Before Roosevelt's death, Harriman had cabled: "It may be difficult . . . to believe, but it still may be true that Stalin and Molotov considered at Yalta that by our willingness to accept a general wording of the declaration on Poland and liberated Europe, by our recognition of the need of the Red Army for security behind its lines, and of the predominant interest of Russia in Poland as a friendly neighbor and as a corridor to Germany, we understood and were ready to accept Soviet policies already known to us."

Harriman wanted the American government to select a few test cases and make the Russians realize they could not continue their present policies. Such tactics, he advised, would place Russian-American relations on a more realistic basis and compel the Soviet Union to adhere to the American interpretation of the issues in dispute. Because the Soviet government "needed our [economic assistance] . . . in their reconstruction," and because Stalin did not wish to break with the United States, Harriman thought Truman "could stand firm on important issues without running serious risks." As early as January 1944 Harriman had emphasized that "the Soviet Government places the utmost importance on our cooperation" in providing economic assistance, and he had concluded: "it is a factor which should be integrated into the fabric of our overall relations." In early April Harriman had proposed that unless the United States were prepared "to live in a world dominated largely by Soviet influence, we must use our economic power to assist those countries that are naturally friendly to our concepts." In turn, he had recommended "tying our economic assistance directly into our political problems with the Soviet Union."

General George Marshall, the Army Chief of Staff, and Secretary of War Henry Stimson, however, recommended caution. Stimson observed "that the Russians perhaps were being more realistic than we were in regard to their own security," and he feared "that we would find ourselves breaking our relations

with Russia on the most important and difficult question which we and Russia
have gotten between us." Leahy, though supporting a firm policy, admitted
that the Yalta agreement "was susceptible to two interpretations." Secretary of
State Edward Stettinius read aloud the Yalta decision and concluded "that this
was susceptible of only one interpretation."

Having heard his advisers' arguments, Truman resolved to force the Polish
question: to impose his interpretation of the Yalta agreement even if it destroyed
the United Nations. He later explained that this was the test of Russian
cooperation. If Stalin would not abide by his agreements, the U.N. was doomed,
and, anyway, there would not be enough enthusiasm among the American
electorate to let the United States join the world body. "Our agreements with
the Soviet Union so far . . . [have] been a one-way street." That could not
continue, Truman told his advisers. "If the Russians did not wish to join us,
they could go to hell." ("FDR's appeasement of Russia is over," joyously wrote
Senator Arthur Vandenberg, the Republican leader on foreign policy.)
Continuing in this spirit at a private conference with Molotov, the new President
warned that economic aid would depend upon Russian behavior in fulfilling the
Yalta agreement. Brushing aside the diplomat's contention that the
Anglo-American interpretation of the Yalta agreement was wrong, the President
accused the Russians of breaking agreements and scolded the Russian Foreign
Minister. When Molotov replied, "I have never been talked to like that in my
life," Truman warned him, "Carry out your agreement and you won't get talked
to like that."

At the United Nations conference in San Francisco, when Anthony Eden, the
British Foreign Minister, saw a copy of Truman's "blunt message" about Poland
to Stalin, "he could scarcely believe his eyes . . . and cheered loudly," reported
Vandenberg. But the policy of firmness was not immediately successful.
American-Russian relations were further strained by the disputes at the meeting
to create the U.N.—over the veto, the admission of fascist Argentina, and the
persistent question of Poland. Despite Soviet objections and Roosevelt's promise
at Yalta to exclude Argentina from the U.N., the United States supported the
Latin American state's candidacy for membership. In committee Molotov, whom
Stalin had sent to establish good will with the new President, tried to block the
admission of Argentina until the Lublin Poles were also admitted, but his
proposed bargain was overwhelmingly defeated. Later in the plenary session,
when only three nations voted with Russia, the Soviets found additional evidence
for their fears of an American bloc directed against their interests. The Truman
administration's action also gave the Soviets more reason to doubt America's
explanations that her interests in Poland were inspired simply by a desire to
guarantee representative, democratic governments. Moreover, because of the
American bloc and Soviet fears that the U.N. (like the League of Nations) might
be used against her, Molotov was at first unwilling to accede to the demands of
the United States and the smaller nations who wished to exclude procedural
questions before the Security Council from the great power veto.

The Soviets were further embittered when the United States abruptly curtailed
lend-lease six days after V-E Day. Though Truman later explained this
termination as simply a "mistake," as policy-making by subordinates, his

recollection was incomplete and wrong. Leo Crowley, the director of lend-lease, and Joseph Grew, the Under Secretary of State, the two subordinates most closely involved, had repeatedly warned the President of the likely impact of such action on relations with Russia, and the evidence suggests that the government, as Harriman had counseled, was seeking to use economic power to achieve diplomatic means. Termination of lend-lease, Truman later wrote, "should have been done on a gradual basis which would not have made it appear as if somebody had been deliberately snubbed." Yet, despite this later judgment, Truman had four days after signing the order in which to modify it before it was to be implemented and announced, and the lend-lease administrator (in the words of Grew) had made "sure that the President understands the situation." The administrator knew "that we would be having difficulty with the Russians and did not want them to be running all over town for help." After discussing the decision with Truman, Grew, presumably acting with the President's approval, had even contrived to guarantee that curtailment would be a dramatic shock. When the Soviet chargé d'affaires had telephoned Grew the day before the secret order was to become effective, the Under Secretary had falsely denied that lend-lease to Russia was being halted. Harriman, according to Grew's report to the Secretary of State, "said that we would be getting 'a good tough slashback' from the Russians but that we would have to face it."

Presumably to patch the alliance, Truman dispatched to Moscow Harry Hopkins, Roosevelt's former adviser and a staunch advocate of Soviet-American friendship. Hopkins denied that Truman's action was an American effort to demonstrate economic power and coerce Russia ("pressure on the Russians to soften them up," as Stalin charged). Instead he emphasized that "Poland had become a symbol of our ability to work out our problems with the Soviet Union." Stalin acknowledged "the right of the United States as a world power to participate in the Polish question," but he stressed the importance of Poland to Soviet security. Within twenty-five years the "Germans had twice invaded Russia via Poland," he emphasized. "All the Soviet Union wanted was that Poland should not be in a position to open the gates to Germany," and that required a government friendly to Russia. There was "no intention," he promised, "to interfere in Poland's internal affairs" or to Sovietize Poland.

Through the Hopkins mission, Truman and Stalin reached a compromise: 70 per cent of the new Polish government (fourteen of twenty ministers) should be drawn from the Lublin Committee. At the time there was reason to believe that such heavy communist influence would not lead to Soviet control. Stalin had reaffirmed the pledge of free elections in Poland, and Stanislaw Mikolajczyk, former Prime Minister of the exile government in London and Deputy Prime Minister in the new coalition government, was optimistic. He hoped (in Harriman's words) that "a reasonable degree of freedom and independence can be preserved now and that in time after conditions in Europe can become more stable and [as] Russia turns her attention to her internal development, controls will be relaxed and Poland will be able to gain for herself her independence of life as a nation even though he freely accepts that Poland's security and foreign policy must follow the lead of Moscow."

Truman compromised and soon recognized the new Polish government, but he did not lose his hopes of rolling back the Soviets from their spheres of influence in Eastern Europe. Basing most of his case on the Yalta "Declaration on Liberated Europe" (for which he relied on State Department interpretations), Truman hoped to force Russia to permit representative governments in its zones, and expected that free elections would diminish, perhaps even remove, Soviet authority. Refusing to extend diplomatic recognition to Rumania and Bulgaria, he emphasized that these governments were "neither representative of nor responsive to the will of the people."

"The opportunities for the democratic elements in Rumania and Bulgaria are not less than, say, in Italy, with which the Governments of the United States and the Soviet Union have already resumed diplomatic relations," replied Stalin, who was willing to exaggerate to emphasize his case. The Russians were demanding a *quid pro quo,* and they would not yield. At Potsdam, in late July, when Truman demanded "immediate reorganization" of the governments of Hungary and Bulgaria to "include representatives of all significant democratic elements" and three-power assistance in "holding . . . free and unfettered elections," Stalin pointed to Greece, again to remind Truman of the earlier agreements. The Russians were "not meddling in Greek affairs," he noted, adding that the Bulgarian and Rumanian governments were fulfilling the armistice agreements while in Greece "terrorism rages . . . against democratic elements." (One member of the American delegation later claimed that Stalin at one point made his position clear, stating that "any freely elected government [in Eastern Europe] would be anti-Soviet and that we cannot permit.") In effect, Stalin demanded that the United States abide by his construction of earlier agreements, and that Truman acknowledge what Roosevelt had accepted as the terms of the sphere-of-influence agreements—that democratic forms and anti-communist democrats of Eastern Europe be abandoned to the larger cause of Russian-American concord.

Though the Allies at Potsdam were not able to settle the dispute over influence in Eastern Europe, they did reach a limited agreement on other European issues. In a "package" deal the Soviets accepted Italy in the U.N. after a peace treaty could be arranged; the United States and Great Britain agreed to set the temporary western border of Poland at the Oder-Neisse line; and the Soviets settled for far less in reparations than they had expected. The decisions on Germany were the important settlements, and the provision on reparations, when linked with American avoidance of offering Russia economic aid, left Russia without the assistance she needed for the pressing task of economic reconstruction.

Russia had long been seeking substantial economic aid, and the American failure to offer it seemed to be part of a general strategy. Earlier Harriman had advised "that the development of friendly relations [with Russia] would depend upon a generous credit," and recommended "that the question of the credit should be tied into our overall diplomatic relations with the Soviet Union and at the appropriate time the Russians should be given to understand that our willingness to cooperate wholeheartedly with them in their vast reconstruction problem will depend upon their behavior in international matters." In January 1945 Roosevelt had decided not to discuss at Yalta the $6 billion credit to the

Soviet Union, explaining privately, "I think it's very important that we hold this back and don't give them any promises until we get what we want." (Secretary Morgenthau, in vigorous disagreement, believed that both the President and Secretary of State Stettinius were wrong, and "that if they wanted to get the Russians to do something they should . . . do it nice. . . . Don't drive such a hard bargain that when you come through it does not taste good.") In future months American officials continued to delay, presumably using the prospect of a loan for political leverage. Shortly before Potsdam, the administration had secured congressional approval for a $1 billion loan fund which could have been used to assist Russia, but the issue of "credits to the Soviet Union" apparently was never even discussed.

Shunting aside the loan, the United States also retreated from Roosevelt's implied agreement at Yalta that reparations would be about $20 billion (half of which the Soviets would receive); Truman's new Secretary of State, James F. Byrnes, pointed out that the figures were simply the "basis" for discussion. (He was technically correct, but obviously Roosevelt had intended it as a general promise and Stalin had so understood it. Had it not been so intended, why had Churchill refused to endorse this section of the Yalta agreement?) Because Byrnes was unwilling to yield, the final agreement on reparations was similar to the terms that would have prevailed if there had been no agreement: the Soviet Union would fill her claims largely by removals from her own zone. That was the substance of the Potsdam agreement. The Russians also surrendered any hopes of participating in control of the heavily industrialized Ruhr, and confirmed the earlier retreat from the policy of dismemberment of Germany. They settled for an agreement that they could trade food and raw materials from their zone for 15 per cent of such industrial capital equipment from the Western Zones "as is unnecessary for the German peace economy," and that the allies would transfer from the Western Zones "10 per cent of such industrial capital equipment as is unnecessary for the German peace economy"—but the agreement left undefined what was necessary for the economy.

Potsdam, like Yalta, left many of the great questions unresolved. "One fact that stands out more clearly than others is that nothing is ever settled," wrote Lord Alanbrooke, Chief of the British Staff, in his diary. As he observed, neither the United States nor Russia had yielded significantly. Russia had refused to move from the areas that her armies occupied, and the United States had been vigorous in her efforts, but without offering economic assistance to gain concessions. Though the atomic bomb may not have greatly influenced Truman's actions in the months before Potsdam, the bomb certainly influenced his behavior at Potsdam. When he arrived he still wanted (and expected) Russian intervention in the Japanese war. During the conference he learned about the successful test at Alamogordo. With Russian intervention no longer necessary, Truman's position hardened noticeably. As sole possessor of the bomb, he had good reason to expect easier future dealings with Stalin. For months Stimson had been counseling that the bomb would be the "master card," and Truman, acting on Stimson's advice, even delayed the Potsdam Conference until a time when he would know about the bomb. On the eve of the conference the President had confided to an adviser, "If it explodes, as I think it will, I'll certainly have a hammer on those boys [the Russians]."

At Potsdam President Truman was "delighted" when Stimson brought him the news about the bomb on July 16. Upon learning more about the results of the test, Truman (according to Stimson) said "it gave him an entirely new feeling of confidence and he thanked me for having come to the conference and being present to help him in this way." The President's enthusiasm and new sense of power were soon apparent in his meetings with the other heads of state, for as Churchill notes (in Stimson's words), "Truman was evidently much fortified by something that had happened and . . . he stood up to the Russians in a most emphatic and decisive manner." After reading the full report on the Alamogordo explosion, Churchill said, "Now I know what happened to Truman yesterday. I couldn't understand it. When he got to the meeting after having read this report he was a changed man. He told the Russians just where they got off and generally bossed the whole meeting."

"From that moment [when we learned of the successful test] our outlook on the future was transformed," Churchill explained later. Forced earlier to concede parts of Eastern Europe to the Russians because Britain did not have the power to resist Soviet wishes and the United States had seemed to lack the desire, Churchill immediately savored the new possibilities. The Prime Minister (Lord Alanbrooke wrote in his diary about Churchill's enthusiasm) "was completely carried away . . . we now had something in our hands which would redress the balance with the Russians. The secret of this explosive and the power to use it would completely alter the diplomatic equilibrium. . . . Now we had a new value which redressed our position (pushing out his chin and scowling); now we could say, 'If you insist on doing this or that well . . . And then where were the Russians!' "

Stimson and Byrnes had long understood that the bomb could influence future relations with Russia, and, after the successful test, they knew that Russian entry was no longer necessary to end the Japanese war. Upon Truman's direction, Stimson conferred at Potsdam with General Marshall and reported to the President that Marshall no longer saw a need for Russian intervention. "It is quite clear," cabled Churchill from Potsdam, "that the United States do not at the present time desire Russian participation in the war against Japan."

"The new explosive alone was sufficient to settle matters," Churchill reported. The bomb had displaced the Russians in the calculations of American policy-makers. The combat use of the bomb, then, was not viewed as the only way to end the Far Eastern war promptly. In July there was ample evidence that there were other possible strategies—a noncombat demonstration, a warning, a blockade. Yet, before authorizing the use of the bomb at Hiroshima, Truman did not try *any* of the possible strategies, including the three most likely: guaranteeing the position of the Japanese Emperor (and hence making surrender conditional), seeking a Russian declaration of war (or announcement of intent), or waiting for Russian entry into the war.

As an invasion of the Japanese mainland was not scheduled until about November 1, and as Truman knew that the Japanese were sending out "peace feelers" and that the main obstacle to peace seemed to be the requirement of unconditional surrender (which threatened the position of the Emperor), he could wisely have revised the terms of surrender. At first Under Secretary of State Grew and then Stimson had urged Truman earlier to revise the terms in this way, and he had been sympathetic. But at Potsdam Stimson found that Truman and Byrnes had rejected his advice. As a result the proclamation issued from Potsdam by the United States, Great Britain, and China retained the demand for unconditional surrender when a guarantee of the Emperor's government might have removed the chief impediment to peace.

Nor was Truman willing to seek a Russian declaration of war (or even an announcement of intent). Even though American advisers had long believed that the *threat* of Russian entry might be sufficient to compel Japanese capitulation, Truman did not invite Stalin to sign the proclamation, which would have constituted a statement of Russian intent. There is even substantial evidence that Truman sought to delay Russian entry into the war.

Pledging to maintain the position of the Emperor, seeking a Russian declaration of war (or announcement of intent), awaiting Russian entry—each of these options, as well as others, had been proposed in the months before Hiroshima and Nagasaki. Each was available to Truman. Why did he not try one or more? No *definite* answer is possible. But it is clear that Truman was either incapable or unwilling to reexamine his earlier assumption (or decision) of using the bomb. Under the tutelage of Byrnes and Stimson, Truman had come to assume by July that the bomb should be used, and perhaps he was incapable of reconsidering this strategy because he found no compelling reason not to use the bomb. Or he may have consciously rejected the options because he wanted to use the bomb. Perhaps he was vindictive and wished to retaliate for Pearl Harbor and other atrocities. (In justifying the use of the bomb against the Japanese, he wrote a few days after Nagasaki, "The only language they seem to understand is the one we have been using to bombard them. When you have to deal with a beast you have to treat him as a beast.") Or, most likely, Truman agreed with Byrnes that using the bomb would advance other American policies: it would end the war before the Russians could gain a hold in Manchuria, it would permit the United States to exclude Russia from the occupation government of Japan, and it would make the Soviets more manageable in Eastern Europe. It would enable the United States to shape the peace according to its own standards.

At minimum, then, the use of the bomb reveals the moral insensitivity of the President—whether he used it because the moral implications did not compel a reexamination of assumptions, or because he sought retribution, or because he sought to keep Russia out of Manchuria and the occupation government of Japan, and to make her more manageable in Eastern Europe. In 1945 American foreign policy was not innocent, nor was it unconcerned about Russian power, nor did it assume that the United States lacked the power to impose its will on the Russian state, nor was it characterized by high moral purpose or consistent dedication to humanitarian principles.

Both Secretary of War Stimson and Secretary of State Byrnes had foreseen the importance of the bomb to American foreign policy. To Stimson it had long promised to be the "master card" for diplomacy. After Hiroshima and Nagasaki

Byrnes was eager to use the bomb as at least an "implied threat" in
negotiations with Russia, and Truman seems to have agreed to a vigorous
course in trying to roll back Russian influence in Eastern Europe.

Truman seemed to be rejecting Stimson's recommendations that
international control of atomic energy be traded for important Russian
concessions—"namely the settlement of the Polish, Rumanian, Yugoslavian,
and Manchurian problems." In his report on the Potsdam Conference the day
after the second bomb, the President asserted that Rumania, Bulgaria,
and Hungary "are not to be spheres of influence of any one power" and at the
same time proclaimed that the United States would be the "trustees" of the
atomic bomb.

Following Truman's veiled threat, Byrnes continued his efforts to roll back
the Soviet Union's influence. Assisted by a similar protest by the British,
who clearly recognized the power of the bomb, he gained postponement of the
Bulgarian elections, charging that the government was not "adequately
representative of important elements . . . of democratic opinion" and that its
arrangements for elections "did not insure freedom from the fear of force
or intimidation." In Hungary, Russia also acceded to similar Anglo-American
demands and postponed the scheduled elections. It is not unreasonable to
conclude that the bomb had made the Russians more tractable. "The significance
of Hiroshima was not lost on the Russians," Alexander Werth, British
correspondent in the Soviet Union, later reported. "It was clearly realized that
this was a New Fact in the world's power politics, that the bomb constituted
a threat to Russia. . . . Everybody . . . believed that although the two
[atomic] bombs had killed or maimed [the] . . . Japanese, their real purpose
was, first and foremost, to intimidate Russia."

Perhaps encouraged by his successes in Bulgaria and Hungary, Byrnes "wished
to have the implied threat of the bomb in his pocket during the [September]
conference" of foreign ministers in London. Stimson confided to his diary
that Byrnes "was very much against any attempt to cooperate with Russia. His
mind is full of his problems with the coming meeting . . . and he looks to
having the presence of the bomb in his pocket . . . as a great weapon to get
through the thing he has. He also told me of a number of acts of perfidy . . . of
Stalin which they had encountered at Potsdam and felt in the light of those
that we would not rely upon anything in the way of promises from them."

The London conference ended in deadlock, disbanding without even a joint
communiqué. Despite American possession of the bomb, Molotov would
not yield to American demands to reorganize the governments of Bulgaria and
Rumania. In turn, he demanded for Russia a role in the occupation government
of Japan, but Byrnes rebuffed the proposal. Unprepared for this issue,
Byrnes was also unwilling or unable to understand Soviet anxieties about the
security of their frontiers, and he pressed most vigorously for the reorganization
of the Rumanian government. He would not acknowledge and perhaps
could not understand the dilemma of his policy: that he was supporting free
elections in areas (particularly in Rumania) where the resulting governments
would probably be hostile to the Soviet Union, and yet he was arguing
that democracy in Eastern Europe was compatible with Soviet demands for

security. Unable to accept that Byrnes might be naïve, Molotov questioned the
Secretary's sincerity and charged that he wanted governments unfriendly
to the Soviet Union. From this, Byrnes could only conclude later, "It seemed
that the Soviet Union was determined to dominate Europe."

While the United States in the cases of these Eastern European nations chose
to support traditional democratic principles and neither to acknowledge its
earlier agreements on spheres of influence nor to respect Russian fears, Byrnes
would not admit the similarity between Russian behavior in Rumania and
British action in Greece. As part of the terms of his agreement with Churchill,
Stalin had allowed the British to suppress a revolutionary force in Greece,
and as a result the Greek government could not be accurately interpreted as
broadly representative nor as a product of democratic procedures. Yet, as
Molotov emphasized, the United States had not opposed British action in Greece
or questioned the legitimacy of that government, nor was the United States
making a reversal of British imperialism in Greece a condition for the
large loan that Britain needed.

Some American observers, however, were aware of this double standard. In
the northern Pacific and in Japan, America was to have the deciding voice,
but in Eastern Europe, emphasized Walter Lippmann, "we invoke the principle
that this is one world in which decisions must not be taken unilaterally."
Most Americans did not see this paradox, and Byrnes probably expressed
crystallizing national sentiment that autumn when he concluded that the dispute
with Russia was a test of whether "we really believed in what we said about
one world and our desire to build collective security, or whether we were willing
to accept the Soviet preference for the simpler task of dividing the world
into two spheres of influence."

Despite Byrnes's views, and although he could not secure a reorganization of
the Rumanian government, communist influence was weakened in other parts
of Eastern Europe. In Budapest free elections were held and the Communist
party was routed; and early in November, just two days after the United States
recognized Hungary, the Communists lost in the national elections there.
In Bulgaria elections took place in "complete order and without disturbance,"
and, despite American protests, a Communist-dominated single ticket
(representing most of the political parties) triumphed.

While the Soviet Union would not generally permit in Eastern Europe
conditions that conformed to Western ideals, Stalin was pursuing a cautious
policy and seeking accommodation with the West. He was willing to
allow capitalism but was suspicious of American efforts at economic penetration
which could lead to political dominance. Though by the autumn of 1945 the
governments in Russia's general area of influence were subservient in foreign
policy, they varied in form and in degree of independence—democracy
in Czechoslovakia (the only country in this area with a democratic tradition),
free elections and the overthrow of the Communist party in Hungary, a
Communist-formed coalition government in Bulgaria, a broadly based but
Communist-dominated government in Poland, and a Soviet-imposed government
in Rumania (the most anti-Russian of these nations). In all of these countries
Communists controlled the ministries of interior (the police) and were
able to suppress anti-Soviet groups, including anti-communist democrats.

Those who have attributed to Russia a policy of inexorable expansion have often neglected this immediate postwar period, or they have interpreted it simply as a necessary preliminary (a cunning strategy to allay American suspicions until the American Army demobilized and left the continent) to the consolidation and extension of power in east-central Europe. From this perspective, however, much of Stalin's behavior becomes strangely contradictory and potentially self-defeating. If he had planned to create puppets rather than an area of "friendly governments," why (as Isaac Deutscher asks) did Stalin "so stubbornly refuse to make any concessions to the Poles over their eastern frontiers?" Certainly, also, his demand for reparations from Hungary, Rumania, and Bulgaria would have been unnecessary if he had planned to take over these countries. (America's insistence upon using a loan to Russia to achieve political goals, and the nearly twenty-month delay after Russia first submitted a specific proposal for assistance, led Harriman to suggest in November that the loan policy "may have contributed to their [Russian] avaricious policies in the countries occupied or liberated by the Red Army.")

Russian sources are closed, so it is not possible to prove that Soviet intentions were conservative; nor for the same reason is it possible for those who adhere to the thesis of inexorable Soviet expansion to prove their theory. But the available evidence better supports the thesis that these years should be viewed not as a cunning preliminary to the harshness of 1947 and afterward, but as an attempt to establish a *modus vivendi* with the West and to protect "socialism in one country." This interpretation explains more adequately why the Russians delayed nearly three years before ending dissent and hardening policies in the countries behind their own military lines. It would also explain why the Communist parties in France and Italy were cooperating with the coalition governments until these parties were forced out of the coalitions in 1947. The American government had long hoped for the exclusion of these Communist parties, and in Italy, at least, American intimations of greater economic aid to a government without Communists was an effective lever. At the same time Stalin was seeking to prevent the revolution in Greece.

If the Russian policy was conservative and sought accommodation (as now seems likely), then its failure must be explained by looking beyond Russian actions. Historians must reexamine this period and reconsider American policies. Were they directed toward compromise? Can they be judged as having sought adjustment? Or did they demand acquiescence to the American world view, thus thwarting real negotiations?

There is considerable evidence that American actions clearly changed after Roosevelt's death. Slowly abandoning the tactics of accommodation, they became even more vigorous after Hiroshima. The insistence upon rolling back Soviet influence in Eastern Europe, the reluctance to grant a loan for Russian reconstruction, the inability to reach an agreement on Germany, the maintenance of the nuclear monopoly—all of these could have contributed to the sense of Russian insecurity. The point, then, is that in 1945 and 1946 there may still have been possibilities for negotiations and settlements, for accommodations and adjustments, if the United States had been willing to recognize Soviet fears, to accept Soviet power in her areas of influence, and to ease anxieties.

two
a defense of
american policy

JOHN LEWIS GADDIS

*John Lewis Gaddis received his Ph.D. from the University
of Texas in 1968 and is an associate professor of
history at Ohio University.* The United States and the
Origins of the Cold War, 1941–1947 *provides the most
comprehensive statement of American-Russian relations
from the development of the wartime coalition to the
beginning of the containment policy. Basing his
study on extensive use of primary sources, Professor Gaddis
challenges the revisionists' emphasis on the economic
orientation of American diplomacy and suggests that policy
was determined by a variety of forces and circumstances.
Can his criticism of the revisionists be applied fairly
to the Bernstein article? How do Bernstein and Gaddis
interpret the options of American leaders? Does the
Soviet system, as Gaddis argues, provide its leaders with
greater maneuverability on the international scene
than their American counterparts?*

American leaders did not want a Cold War, but they
wanted insecurity even less. By early 1946, President
Truman and his advisers had reluctantly concluded that
recent actions of the Soviet Union endangered the security
of the United States. This decision grew out of a complex
of internal and external pressures, all filtered through the
perceptions and preconceptions of the men who made
American foreign policy. In order to understand how they
came to this conclusion, it is necessary to view the situation
as they saw it, not as it appears today in the cold, but not
always clear, light of historical hindsight.

Source: John Lewis Gaddis, *The United States and the Origins
of the Cold War, 1941–1947* (New York: Columbia
University Press, 1972), pp. 353–61. Reprinted by permission
of the publisher.

World War II had produced a revolution in United States foreign policy. Prior to that conflict, most Americans believed that their country could best protect itself by minimizing political entanglements overseas. Events of 1939–40 persuaded leaders of the Roosevelt Administration that they had been wrong; Pearl Harbor convinced remaining skeptics. From then on, American policy-makers would seek security through involvement, not isolation: to prevent new wars, they believed, the whole system of relations between nations would have to be reformed. Assuming that only their country had the power and influence to carry out this task, United States officials set to work, even before formal entry into the war, to plan a peace settlement which would accomplish such a reformation.

Lessons of the past greatly influenced Washington's vision of the future. Determined to avoid mistakes which, in their view, had caused World War II, American planners sought to disarm defeated enemies, give peoples of the world the right to shape their own future, revive world trade, and replace the League of Nations with a new and more effective collective security organization. But without victory over the Axis, the United States would never have the opportunity to implement its plan for peace. Given the realities of the military situation, victory depended upon cooperation with the Soviet Union, an ally whose commitment to American postwar ideals was, at best, questionable.

Kremlin leaders, too, looked to the past in planning for the future, but their very different experiences led them to conclusions not always congruent with those of their American allies. For Stalin, the key to peace was simple: keep Russia strong and Germany weak. The Soviet dictator enthusiastically applauded American insistence on unconditional surrender, questioning only the wisdom of making this policy public. He showed little interest in Washington's plans for collective security, the reduction of tariff barriers, and reform of the world monetary system. Self-determination in Eastern Europe, however, he would not allow: the region was vital to Soviet security, but the people who lived there were bitterly anti-Russian. Nor could Stalin view with equanimity Allied efforts, also growing out of lessons of the past, to limit reparations removals from Germany. These two conflicts—Eastern Europe and Germany—became major areas of contention in the emerging Cold War.

Moscow's position would not have seemed so alarming to American officials, however, had it not been for the Soviet Union's continued commitment to an ideology dedicated to the overthrow of capitalism throughout the world. Hopes that the United States might cooperate successfully with the USSR after the war had been based on the belief, encouraged by Stalin himself, that the Kremlin had given up its former goal of exporting communism. Soviet expansion into Eastern Europe in 1944 and 1945, together with the apparent abandonment of popular front tactics by the world communist movement, caused Western observers to fear that they had been misled. Just at the moment of victory over the Axis, the old specter of world revolution reappeared.

It seems likely that Washington policy-makers mistook Stalin's determination to ensure Russian security through spheres of influence for a renewed effort to spread communism outside the borders of the Soviet Union. The Russians did not immediately impose communist regimes on all the countries they occupied

after the war, and Stalin showed notoriously little interest in promoting
the fortunes of communist parties in areas beyond his control. But the Soviet
leader failed to make the limited nature of his objectives clear. Having just
defeated one dictator thought to have had unlimited ambitions, Americans
could not regard the emergence of another without the strongest feelings of
apprehension and anger.

Nor did they see any reason to acquiesce timidly in what Stalin seemed to be
doing. The United States had come out of the war with a monopoly over the
world's most powerful weapon, the atomic bomb, and a near-monopoly over the
productive facilities which could make possible quick rehabilitation of
war-shattered economies. Convinced that technology had given them the means
to shape the postwar order to their liking, Washington officials assumed that
these instruments would leave the Russians no choice but to comply with
American peace plans. Attempts to extract concessions from Moscow in return
for a loan failed, however, when the Soviet Union turned to German
reparations to meet its reconstruction needs. The Russians also refused to be
impressed by the atomic bomb, leaving the Truman Administration with
the choice of actually using it, or returning to *quid pro quo* bargaining. American
omnipotence turned out to be an illusion because Washington policy-makers
failed to devise strategies for applying their newly gained power effectively in
practical diplomacy.

Frustrated in their efforts to work out an acceptable settlement with the USSR,
under severe pressure from Congress and the public to make no further
compromises, American leaders embarked on a new Russian policy during the
first months of 1946. Henceforth, expansionist moves by the Kremlin
would be resisted, even at the risk of war. Negotiations would continue, but
future concessions would have to come from Moscow. Meanwhile, the United
States would begin rebuilding its military forces, now badly depleted by
demobilization, and would launch an ambitious program of economic assistance
to nations threatened by communism. Administration officials found it
necessary to exaggerate the Soviet ideological challenge in order to win support
for these projects from parsimonious legislators, but there can be no doubt
that the President and his advisers regarded the danger as a serious one. Nor can
there be any question that the general principle of "getting tough with
Russia" evoked overwhelming public approval: a generation seared by the
memory of Munich would not tolerate appeasement, however unpleasant the
alternatives might be.

It is easy for historians, writing a quarter of a century later, to suggest ways
in which the United States might have avoided, or at least lessened, the dangers
of a postwar confrontation with the Soviet Union. President Roosevelt could
have eased Russia's military burden by launching a second front in Europe
in 1942 or 1943. He could have explicitly exempted Eastern Europe from
provisions of the Atlantic Charter, thereby recognizing the Soviet sphere of
influence in that part of the world. American officials could have aided in the
massive task of repairing Russian war damage by granting a generous
reconstruction loan, and by allowing extensive reparations removals from
Germany. Finally, the United States could have attempted to allay

Soviet distrust by voluntarily relinquishing its monopoly over the atomic bomb.

But these were not viable alternatives at the time. A premature second front would have greatly increased American casualties and might have weakened support for the war effort. Recognition of the Soviet position in Eastern Europe would have aroused opposition in the Senate to American membership in the United Nations, and might have endangered Roosevelt's reelection prospects. Economic concessions to the Russians, in the form of either a reconstruction loan or a more flexible attitude on reparations, would have evoked a storm of protest from a Congress still largely isolationist in its approach to foreign aid. A decision to give up the atomic bomb would have so alienated the American people and their representatives on Capitol Hill as to impair the very functioning of the government. Policy-makers operate within a certain range of acceptable options, but they, not historians, define degrees of acceptability. It is surely uncharitable, if not unjust, to condemn officials for rejecting courses of action which, to them, seemed intolerable.

A fairer approach is to ask why policy-makers defined their alternatives so narrowly. Important recent work by revisionist historians suggests that requirements of the economic system may have limited the options open to American officials in seeking an accommodation with Russia. Leaders of the United States had become convinced, revisionists assert, that survival of the capitalist system at home required the unlimited expansion of American economic influence overseas. For this reason, the United States could not recognize legitimate Soviet interests in Eastern Europe, Germany, or elsewhere. By calling for an international "open door" policy, Washington had projected its interests on a worldwide scale. The real or imagined threat of communism anywhere endangered these interests, and had to be contained.

Revisionists are correct in emphasizing the importance of internal constraints, but they have defined them too narrowly: by focusing so heavily on economics, they neglect the profound impact of the domestic political system on the conduct of American foreign policy. The Constitution did, after all, give the public and their representatives on Capitol Hill at least a negative influence in this field, and while these influences may not have determined the specific direction of diplomatic initiatives, they did impose definite limitations on how far policy-makers could go. The delay in opening the second front, nonrecognition of Moscow's sphere of influence in Eastern Europe, the denial of economic aid to Russia, and the decision to retain control of the atomic bomb can all be explained far more plausibly by citing the Administration's need to maintain popular support for its policies rather than by dwelling upon requirements of the economic order.

One might, of course, argue that the political system reflected the economic substructure, and that American officials were merely unwitting tools of capitalism, but it is difficult to justify this assumption without resorting to the highly questionable techniques of economic determinism. At times, it seems as if revisionists do employ this approach—they frequently take literally only statements of economic interest, disregarding as irrelevant whatever other explanations policy-makers gave for their actions. But the revisionists are not consistent in their economic determinism. Carried to its logical conclusion, that view of history would seem to indicate that the Cold War was an irrepressible conflict between two diametrically opposed ideologies; a clash for which individuals, presumably puppets of these systems, could bear no responsibility. Revisionists do not see the Cold War that way. They assert that the United States, because of its military and economic superiority over the Soviet Union, could have accepted Moscow's postwar demands without endangering American security. Because it did not, they hold leaders of the United States responsible for the way in which the Cold War developed, if not for the Cold War itself. This places revisionists in the odd position of employing a single-cause explanation of human behavior, yet criticizing the subjects they deal with for not liberating themselves from the mechanistic framework which they, as historians, have imposed.

But even if, as the revisionists suggest, American officials had enjoyed a completely free hand in seeking a settlement with the Soviet Union, it seems unlikely that they would have succeeded. Accomplishment of this task required not only conciliatory actions by Washington but a receptive attitude on the part of Moscow. The latter simply did not exist. Traditional distrust of foreigners, combined with ideological differences, would have militated against a relationship of mutual trust with the United States regardless of who ruled Russia. Stalin's paranoia, together with the bureaucracy of institutionalized suspicion with which he surrounded himself, made the situation much worse. Information on the internal workings of the Soviet government during this period is still sparse, but sufficient evidence exists to confirm the accuracy of Kennan's 1946 conclusion that Russian hostility sprang chiefly from internal sources not susceptible to gestures of conciliation from the West.

Historians have debated at length the question of who caused the Cold War, but without shedding much light on the subject. Too often they view that event exclusively as a series of actions by one side and reactions by the other. In fact, policy-makers in both the United States and the Soviet Union were constantly weighing each other's intentions, as they perceived them, and modifying their own courses of action accordingly. In addition, officials in Washington and Moscow brought to the task of policy formulation a variety of preconceptions, shaped by personality, ideology, political pressures, even ignorance and irrationality, all of which influenced their behavior. Once this complex interaction of stimulus and response is taken into account, it becomes clear that neither side can bear sole responsibility for the onset of the Cold War.

But neither should the conflict be seen as irrepressible, if for no other reason than the methodological impossibility of "proving" inevitability in history. The power vacuum in central Europe caused by Germany's collapse made a Russian-American confrontation likely; it did not make it inevitable. Men as well as circumstances make foreign policy, and through such drastic expedients as war, appeasement, or resignation, policy-makers can always alter difficult situations in which they find themselves. One may legitimately ask why they do not choose to go this far, but to view their actions as predetermined by blind, impersonal "forces" is to deny the complexity and particularity of human

behavior, not to mention the ever-present possibility of accident. The
Cold War is too complicated an event to be discussed in terms of either national
guilt or the determinism of inevitability.

If one must assign responsibility for the Cold War, the most meaningful way
to proceed is to ask which side had the greater opportunity to accommodate
itself, at least in part, to the other's position, given the range of alternatives as
they appeared at the time. Revisionists have argued that American policy-makers
possessed greater freedom of action, but their view ignores the constraints
imposed by domestic politics. Little is known even today about how Stalin defined
his options, but it does seem safe to say that the very nature of the Soviet
system afforded him a larger selection of alternatives than were open to leaders
of the United States. The Russian dictator was immune from pressures of
Congress, public opinion, or the press. Even ideology did not restrict him: Stalin
was the master of communist doctrine, not a prisoner of it, and could modify or
suspend Marxism-Leninism whenever it suited him to do so. This is not to
say that Stalin wanted a Cold War—he had every reason to avoid one.
But his absolute powers did give him more chances to surmount the internal
restraints on his policy than were available to his democratic counterparts in the
West.

The Cold War grew out of a complicated interaction of external and internal
developments inside both the United States and the Soviet Union. The
external situation—circumstances beyond the control of either power—left
Americans and Russians facing one another across prostrated Europe at the end
of World War II. Internal influences in the Soviet Union—the search for
security, the role of ideology, massive postwar reconstruction needs, the
personality of Stalin—together with those in the United States—the ideal of
self-determination, fear of communism, the illusion of omnipotence fostered by
American economic strength and the atomic bomb—made the resulting
confrontation a hostile one. Leaders of both superpowers sought peace, but in
doing so yielded to considerations which, while they did not precipitate war,
made a resolution of differences impossible.

three
containment as
a response to
european crises

HERBERT FEIS

*The American response to Soviet aggressiveness, seen in
the traditional accounts of the Cold War, crystallized
in 1947–48 with the promulgation of the Truman Doctrine
and the launching of the Marshall Plan. In* From
Trust to Terror *(1970), Herbert Feis defended
containment as an appropriate and measured policy. Feis
(1893–1972) had a long and distinguished career as
an academician, government servant, and writer. Having
received his Ph.D. in economics from Harvard University
in 1921, Feis taught economics for several years and
wrote on the subject of labor relations and international
trade. From 1931 to 1943, he was an adviser on
economic affairs for the Department of State; in 1944,
he became a special consultant to the secretary of war, a
position he held until 1946. After World War II,
Feis was engaged primarily in research on American
diplomacy during the 1940s. For his several books—which
include* Road to Pearl Harbor *(1950),* The China Tangle
(1953), Churchill, Roosevelt, and Stalin *(1957),*
Between War and Peace *(1960), and* Japan Subdued
*(1961)—Feis was accorded the status of a semiofficial
historian; he was granted access to documents not then
available to other scholars, and his works defended
American policy. From* Trust to Terror *was written without
special considerations, however, and while generally*

Source: Herbert Feis, *From Trust to Terror: The Onset of the
Cold War, 1945–1950* (New York: W. W. Norton, 1970),
pp. 187–95, 197–98, 204–5, 227–28, 238–49. Copyright
© 1970 by Herbert Feis. Reprinted by permission of W. W.
Norton & Company, Inc.

*sympathetic to American policy, Feis is critical of certain aspects. Did
containment represent, from the Soviet view, an act of "trust" or of
"terror"?*

The crisis of decision came abruptly.

Ever since 1820, when Greece had fought for and won independence from
the Ottoman Empire, Great Britain had been its friend and protector. The
enduring admiration for ancient classical Greece in the hearts of English
scholars and statesmen had shed a glow upon the moves of British strategists
and soldiers. But now—in 1947—Britain, itself in a sorry plight, felt compelled
to relinquish the role.

The American Government had several warnings that the Greek Government
was on the verge of collapsing, and it also had indications that the British
Cabinet was going to ask the U.S. to take over. In a memo to Acheson,
Henderson, then Chief of the Near and Middle Eastern Affairs Division, had
described the predicament. Acheson had sent the memo on to Marshall. Before
leaving on February 21st to talk at the bicentennial celebration of Princeton
University, Marshall instructed Acheson to prepare the measures the American
Government might have to take to save the situation in Greece.

Hardly had the Secretary gone, when the British Ambassador in Washington,
Lord Inverchapel (formerly Archibald Clark-Kerr) sent his secretary to the
State Department with a note stating that the British Government must end its
financial support of Greece and begin to withdraw its troops on April 1st. This
had been anxiously discussed by the British Cabinet. It was inspired in part by
the pinch of penury, in part by purpose.

Some permanent officials of the British Foreign Office had argued that this
appeal could be disastrous. The British Ambassador in Athens had warned that
even a whisper of any intention to "cut and run" would cause the Greek
Government to fall. But the Labor Government was tired of expending its
carefully budgeted funds to sustain the situation in Greece—only one of many
external drains. Dalton, the Chancellor of the Exchequer, on hearing the
decision announced over the air, noted in his Diary, "I had been for some time
trying to put an end to the endless dribble of British taxpayers' money to the
Greeks." Bevin had given in to Dalton's importunities. It may be surmised that
he had in mind the possibility of passing the burden and responsibility on to
the United States, thereby ensuring that it would be more surely enmeshed in
the defense of western Europe.

The reaction in Washington was fast and feverish. Secretary Marshall was out
of town. With the stimulus of emergency, Department officials crystalized
their views and ideas and brought them before the State-War-Navy Coordinating
Committee (SWNCC). The Joint Chiefs of Staff, also in an energetic mood,
concurrently discussed the problem. Acheson kept the President and
Marshall advised by telephone of the reports and recommendations that were
being composed.

The American Ambassador in Greece, Lincoln MacVeagh, in well-phrased
messages, stressed the urgency of the situation. So did Paul Porter, who was
head of the American Mission which had been advising the Greek Government

about economic affairs, and Mark Ethridge, who had been sent by Truman to investigate the political turmoil in the Balkans. All three discerned signs of an impending move of the Communists to take over the country. Unless the Greek Government received immediate and enough military and financial aid, they foresaw that it would go down under the effects of surging inflation, strikes, riots, and public panic, giving the Communist guerillas their chance to win control of the country. In the same messages they warned that our aid would not save the situation unless used wisely and honestly. Therefore they recommended that the American Government should stipulate that its aid be administered by an American group large and expert enough, and granted sufficient authority to bring about a thorough reorganization of the Greek economy, public administration, and military direction.

While the American civilian leaders who read these messages from their colleagues in Greece were worrying over the political effect of the downfall of the Greek and Turkish Governments, American military authorities were pondering the strategic consequences. They discerned the possibility that if the Communists secured control of Greece, they might in concert with Bulgaria threaten Turkey and cause it to grant the Soviet Union control of the Dardanelles and a base there. Possibly also the Greek Communists might make Salonika available as a Soviet naval and air base.

Turkey was, our Ambassador in Ankara continued to stress, also vulnerable to Communist agitation and pressure. American assistance was urgently needed for the equipment and enlargement of the army; and beyond that, to shore up the spirit of resistance of the people, and to relieve their poverty.

Marshall was convinced by the reports of our missions in Greece and Turkey, and satisfied with the recommendations of the concerned groups in Washington. Truman agreed that it was vital to American security that the Communists be thwarted in Greece and Turkey. Within hours he approved the proposed program of action.

But he thought with trepidation about what the congressional response might be to the costly hazardous ventures which all those about him were advocating. He therefore asked the two ranking members of the Senate Foreign Relations Committee, Arthur Vandenberg and Tom Connally, and other members of the Congress to meet with Marshall, Acheson, and himself. Admiral Leahy was also present.

Marshall, in his cryptic and dry way, described the situation and explained why he thought it imperative that the United States come to the support of the Greek and Turkish Governments. Incisively, he remarked: "The choice is between acting with energy or losing by default." Most of his auditors were impressed. But some remained unconvinced. They thought the proposed action was not essential to protect American security, being activated rather by Britain's design to salvage its imperial interest. The well-worn question "Aren't we just pulling the British chestnuts out of the fire?" was heard once again.

Acheson took over the presentation. He stretched the panorama of the Communist purpose and saturated it with dread. The Communists, he averred, were trying to get control not only of Greece and Turkey, but of Iran and other Arab countries of the Middle East. They might be on the verge of winning in Italy. They held important places in the French Cabinet; they were extending their area of control in China. If they won in Greece and Turkey, he predicted, it would make it more likely they would win elsewhere—and ultimately everywhere. The fall of the dominoes could be heard as he talked along.

Most of the members of Congress present expressed willingness to support the administration's resolve to aid the Greek and Turkish Governments, quickly and in a substantial way. But the Republican Speaker of the House of Representatives, Joseph Martin, remained opposed, and the Republican Chairman of the Foreign Relations Committee, Senator Vandenberg, did not regard himself as committed.[1] Admiral Leahy, who was against acceptance of the risk and responsibility, recounted in his Diary, "The consensus of opinion of the members of Congress present was that such action could obtain the support of the American people only by a frank, open, public announcement that the action was taken for the purpose of preventing an overthrow of the subject governments by the Communists."

The President's hesitation gave way before his pugnacious streak. He was aroused by the distending challenge of the Communists. To Clark Clifford he remarked he thought it fortunate that the British Government had placed the Greek and Turkish situation "on our doorstep" for if they had not, our response to Communist expansion would have been "too late and too slow."[2]

As advised, he decided that in order to secure approval of the measures he was going to propose, he would have to encase them within a general appeal to ward off Communism.

Some members of the presidential staff were worried. They urged him to have members of the Cabinet test public opinion by preliminary speeches. State Department officials were also disturbed by the possible impact of what Truman had in mind to say and do upon the meeting of the Council of Foreign Ministers that was soon to assemble again at Moscow to discuss peace treaties with Germany and Austria.

[1] In his book *The Crucial Decade*, p. 29, Goldman quotes Vandenberg as saying to Truman: "Mr. President, if that's what you want, there's only one way to get it. That is to make a personal appearance before Congress and scare hell out of the country." Acheson's version of Vandenberg's statement after Acheson finished talking is more restrained. "Mr. President, if you say that to the Congress and the country, I will support you and I believe that most of its members will do the same." Acheson, *Present at the Creation*, p. 219.

[2] Author's talk with Clifford, June 1, 1966.

James Reston, in a well-informed and obviously inspired story he sent from Washington, had explained the turn of official thought clearly. "Through the use of U.S. influence and power in Germany, Austria, Italy and Trieste, naval demonstrations in Greece and in the waters dominating the approach to the Dardanelles; and through the cooperation of the British and some other nations, some kind of balance was achieved . . . but that is threatened by the end of British financial support in Greece." The British and American policy, he observed, was being called in diplomatic circles "stern containment." *New York Times,* March 1, 1946. Reston's use of the term "containment" may have derived from a memorandum by George Kennan, written in February 1946, that was circulating widely and making a strong impression at the time.

Before acting, therefore, Truman called together his Cabinet again, on March 7th, to consider the statement he had in mind to make. He opened the discussion by saying that he knew the question before them was momentous, perhaps as serious as had ever confronted any President. Acheson, in his exposition, admitted that the Greek Government, having many reactionary elements, was not a good government and that the Communist appeals had met response and won followers in Greece because the Greek Government was so corrupt and inefficient. Still, he pressed the point that this small country which had so valiantly resisted Germans and Italians, and was so badly damaged as a consequence, should not be left to succumb to civil war, perhaps Communism. Turkey was regarded as a dependable resistant if encouraged and backed up.

The President was asked by Forrestal (or perhaps by Marx Leva, Forrestal's assistant) whether he really intended to sustain the broad policy being discussed. Were we ready to face the full implications of giving support to free peoples everywhere—in Finland, in China, for example? If not, should not the pertinent sentences be reworded?

All members of the Cabinet agreed that we were engaged in a fundamental struggle and that the Russians would be halted only if stubbornly resisted.

When, three days later (Mar. 10th), the President disclosed his decision and intention to a larger group of influential members of Congress, none spoke in opposition. Vandenberg now said he agreed that, regrettable though it was, it had become necessary to take a public stand against Soviet Communist intrusion into lives of other nations, everywhere. So Truman was assured of Republican approval.

During these same days, with excitement in the air, the work of writing the message which the President was going to send to Congress proceeded. State Department draftsmen consulted constantly with colleagues in the War and Navy Departments, and Averell Harriman, who had succeeded Wallace as Secretary of Commerce, Clark Clifford, and others. Of all the contributors to the drafting, Acheson was the most scintillant and sibilant. His caustic temper, usually well under control, was released by belief that the appeal to the country would have to be spirited and bold. The State Department officer, Joseph Jones, who was the seamstress and custodian of the many drafts, was a crusader, impatient of restraint, and tired of what in his subsequent account he called "the cautious, limited backdoor approach to involvement in world affairs."

Marshall had left on March 5th for the meeting of the Council of Foreign Ministers. It could be foreseen that the message the President was about to send to Congress would offend the Russians. But he had told Acheson and other subordinates to go ahead without regard for the way in which his talks might be affected. While Marshall was en route to Moscow, the text of the Presidential message, which had been given to Clifford by Jones, was sent to him. He answered ". . . questioning the wisdom of this presentation, saying he thought that Truman was overstating the case a bit." The President replied that only by this strong and dramatic statement of the issues could Congress be moved to take the necessary measures.

TRUMAN ADDRESSES CONGRESS

Truman went to the Capital on March 12th to read the message to the two houses of Congress in joint session. Those sections which gave the reasons why the Greek and Turkish people and governments had to be aided and upheld were forcefully matter-of-fact. He sought to meet criticisms before they were made.

What he specifically asked of Congress was to provide authority for assistance to Greece and Turkey in the amount of four hundred million dollars for the period ending June 30, 1948. The sum allocated to Greece would be expended in part for food, clothing, fuel, and seeds, thereby enabling and encouraging industry and farming to revive; and in part to supply and equip the Greek army so it could restore the authority of the Greek Government throughout the country. In the statement of reasons for assisting Turkey, "The integrity [of Turkey] is essential to the preservation of order in the Middle East" was all he said. Strategic considerations were mentioned but not stressed; the emphasis was on the need to improve economic life and social order.

TRUMAN ENUNCIATES A GLOBAL DOCTRINE

These related requests for Greece and Turkey were framed in a broad affirmation of resolve and intention. The message contained an elaboration of American policy of global scope, and called upon the American people to carry an assignment that could be stretched to the furthermost foreign horizon.

One of the primary objectives of American foreign policy, the President said, was ". . . the creation of conditions in which we and other nations will be able to work out a way of life free from coercion. This was a fundamental issue in the war with Germany and Japan." It was one reason the United States had taken a leading part in establishing the United Nations. But this objective would not be realized ". . . unless we are willing to help free peoples to maintain their free institutions and their national integrity against aggressive movements that seek to impose upon them totalitarian regimes."

In other blunt paragraphs he sharply incised an antithesis between Western democratic political ways and institutions, and Communist ones. Because it was doctrinaire, this statement was to be commonly called a "doctrine."

"At the present moment in world history," Truman continued, "nearly every nation must choose between alternative ways of life. The choice is too often not a free one.

"One way of life is based upon the will of the majority, and is distinguished by free institutions, representative government, free elections, guarantees of individual liberty, freedom of speech and religion, and freedom from political oppression.

"The second way of life is based upon the will of a minority forcibly imposed upon the majority. It relies upon terror and oppression, a controlled press and radio, fixed elections, and the suppression of personal freedoms.

"I believe that it must be the policy of the United States to support free peoples who are resisting attempted subjugation by armed minorities or by outside pressures.

"I believe that we must assist free peoples to work out their own destinies in their own way."

Then came one paragraph that could be construed as intended to lessen the qualms of those who feared the assignment would inevitably involve the United States in war in distant regions.

"I believe that our help should be primarily through economic and financial aid which is essential to economic stability and orderly political processes."

What the American Government would do if this kind of aid did not suffice, the President did not forecast. But he tried to give an answer in advance to any who might argue that he was proposing that the United States step in to prevent change anywhere in social situations or relative power relations. In this he repeated in essence what former Secretary of State Byrnes had said in an address to the Overseas Press Club in New York City in February 1946. The Secretary had then remarked: "Though the *status quo* is not sacred and unchallengeable, we cannot overlook a unilateral gnawing away at the *status quo*. The Charter forbids aggression and we cannot allow aggression to be accomplished by coercion or pressure or subterfuges such as political infiltration." The President's explanation was more affirmative, that in preventing changes achieved by these methods in violation of the U.N. Charter, and by helping free and independent nations to maintain their freedom, the United States would be giving effect to the principles of the Charter.

Truman ended with a clarion call: "The seeds of totalitarian regimes are nurtured by misery and want. They spread and grow in the evil soil of poverty and strife. They reach their full growth when the hope of a people for a better life has died. We must keep that hope alive. The free peoples of the world look to us for support in maintaining their freedoms.

"If we falter in our leadership, we may endanger the peace of the world—and we shall surely endanger the welfare of our own nation.

"Great responsibilities have been placed upon us by the swift movement of events.

"I am confident that the Congress will face these responsibilities squarely."

. . . . .

Truman's affirmations marked the fade-out of the vision of a united community of peaceful nations, diverse in social systems and ideals yet all willing to leave others be. Up to then it had still been thought that practitioners of "wars of liberation" would quiet down without being restrained. But now Truman—as flatly and openly as ever Marx and Moscow had spoken out against Capitalist democracies— declared that Communism must be confronted and checked. From then on he seemed to be committing the United States to act in whatever way necessary to foil the wiles and assaults of

Communists upon an independent country. In short, President Truman accepted—it might almost be said reached out to grasp—responsibilities which roamed into the hidden future.

Congress gave Truman a standing ovation. Most Americans found temporary relief for their own exasperation and fears in Truman's blunt challenge to Communism and its agents in many lands. Perhaps some did not realize that it would necessitate great increase in our military forces and readiness to use them when other means failed. Some may have been beguiled by the thought that as sole possessor of atomic weapons, our warnings would be like thunderbolts.

Most European diplomats were amazed by the assertiveness of Truman's message. The tenor of most European comment was gratified but grave.

. . . . .

Before American assistance to Greece could become effective, the situation there became more disturbing. The rebels gained control of a large part of the Pindus and Olympus mountain ranges and nearly all of the northern frontier. The Greek Government fell in dire straits. The following months were tense.

Truman relates that three months later, "on July 16th General Marshall sent me a memorandum on the situation in Greece that began with the words, 'The Greek situation has taken a serious turn in the last three days.' Sizable guerrilla units had crossed the frontier from Albania. It appeared that they were aiming at the occupation of some larger communities that could serve as centers for a 'people's republic.'

"I called the Secretary of the Navy," Truman continues, "and asked him how large a part of our Mediterranean fleet he might be able to move to Greek ports. Secretary Forrestal informed me that it would be entirely practicable to have a large part of the Mediterranean squadron shifted on short order. He expressed a belief that such a visit would have some deterrent effect on the activities of the Communist guerrillas but was unwilling to estimate how the American public might react."

During this period of "touch and go" the administrator of the U.S. aid program in Greece, Dwight Griswold, was organizing a staff, arranging for the reception and distribution of aid supplies, and urging the Greek Government to include new elements and seek the widest possible support.

But the Greek Government was most intent on being enabled to enlarge and equip its army. As Truman remarks in his *Memoirs,* ". . . even as we undertook to bolster the economy of Greece to help her combat Communist agitation, we were faced with her desire to use our aid to further partisan political, rather than national, aims." Griswold was neither an effective administrator nor a persuasive advocate for the distressed Greek workers.

In the agreement with Turkey, signed in July, it was explicitly stipulated that most of the funds provided were to be expended upon its military forces. Local plants producing war materials were to be modernized and enlarged, a net of air fields was to be built, and a great naval base to be established on the Mediterranean coast. A substantial residue was to be used to improve roads and port facilities. Turkey, henceforth, was to be one of our pivotal points of resistance to possible Soviet expansion by subversion or force, or a combination of them.

.   .   .   .   .

In telling of the development of the general theme of global defense of freedom and independence—to deter and counter Communist expansion—I have passed over the one great American initiative to that end.

One passage in Truman's address to Congress on March 12th had forecast it. "The seeds of totalitarian regimes are nurtured by misery and want. They spread and grow in the evil soil of poverty and strife."

The American Government had not been unmindful of the plight of the millions of those left bereft and in distress by the war. In the autumn of 1943 and in 1944 the United States had taken the lead in forming the United Nations Relief and Rehabilitation Administration. This was created to alleviate the need for food, clothing, shelter, medicines, and other forms of relief to millions of these people left destitute as the German and Italian armies retreated: displaced persons, prisoners of war who were freed, forced laborers who were released, former prisoners of concentration camps, and refugees from war-struck areas. To that work of succor, which kept alive and gave a new start to millions of Europeans, the United States had contributed more supplies than all other members together—about 73 percent of the 3 billion dollars' worth from farms, factories, warehouses. Also ours had been the zeal behind the effort to prevent corruption and waste, so that those who needed help were beneficiaries, not middlemen, profiteers, politicians, and bureaucrats. As the endless influx of persons in need and distress swelled, UNRRA funds had run thin, and it was to be closed out June 30, 1947.

During the immediate postwar years, American private capitalists had not dared invest their capital in the damaged and disturbed countries. The financial risks seemed great, inflation was rampant, fiscal collapse possible, and the chances of disorder, civil war, and Communism worrisome. In fact during the period immediately after the war new private American investment in western Europe was less than the European capital that was invested, for safety, in the United States. Private enterprise is attracted by profit, not problems.

Truman, believing himself obligated by the terms of the legislation, had terminated Lend-Lease aid as soon as the war in Europe had ended. He was mindful of the fact that when presiding over the Senate he, himself, on the score that it was unnecessary, had to cast the deciding vote against an amendment that would have explicitly prohibited the President from continuing to provide Lend-Lease assistance.

The British had been told to expect no further assignments of supplies except for use in the war against Japan. Orders to end shipments to the Soviet Union were so worded that ships at sea en route to Russia with Lend-Lease supplies had turned about and unloaded.

In his *Memoirs* Truman explains the decision by a belief that there was a fundamental distinction between the powers that he, as President, could properly exercise in wartime and those he should have in peacetime. In his mind a European recovery program appeared quite different from Lend-Lease—to be dealt with in an entirely different way, in year-by-year consultation with Congress.

Moreover, he thought the interim could be bridged by extending Export-Import Bank credits for United States exports.

. . . . .

The first signal [of a massive economic assistance program] was given by Acheson. On April 7th President Truman had asked him to go as substitute to Cleveland, Mississippi, and speak at the annual meeting of the influential Delta Council. In his ensuing discussions with his staff, some of them, members of groups who had been writing gloomy memos and making gloomier forecasts, impressed upon him how bleak was the situation in Europe and besought him to tell the American people that they might be called on to resume great and sustained support of friendly countries, again in deep trouble. In other words, they urged him to "elaborate the economic intent of the Truman Doctrine."

Sometime soon thereafter (April 15–20) Acheson outlined for the President what he might say. Truman told him to go ahead, and said that he would stand behind the presentation and try to deal with the problem resolutely.

While Acheson's speech was being composed by earnest subordinates, another group was busily trying to formulate a general program for the now recognized emergency. Marshall's frustrating experience in Moscow had convinced him of the need to take measures to deal with the situation in Germany. It was becoming apparent to him that the state of many other western European countries was hardly less "desperate" than that of Germany and that drastic action of wider scope must be taken to enable them to get out of the ditch.

On April 29th the Secretary of State instructed George Kennan to apply his talents to this imperative and constructive task. The Secretary wished to have within a fortnight a paper analyzing the problems of European recovery and recommendations. When, as their brief talk was ending, Kennan asked if there were any more instructions, Marshall said merely: "Avoid trivia." Terseness may be an aid to, or substitute for, thought.

Kennan took up the task eagerly. He, who was closely identified with the policy of "containment" of the Soviet Union, had become, he avers in his *Memoirs,* troubled by the tone of Truman's message to Congress; he was disquieted by the flat portrayal of a world divided between two contrasting ways of life. In this assignment he saw a chance not only to sustain western Europe against the menace of Communism, due to misery and discontent, but also to correct the emphasis of American policy, to shift it from militant challenge to a bid for cooperation to restore the economy of the continent, possibly including the Soviet Union. The swish of doctrine in Truman's message was to be washed away by inundations of generosity.

Acheson spoke on May 8th. The most reverberant passage in this address was: "The war will not be over until the people of the world can again feed and clothe themselves and face the future with some degree of confidence." After reviewing our past considerable essays with facts and reason, he led his audience toward the conclusion that it had become necessary and urgent that the American Government make greater and more comprehensive efforts than it had ever made before in peacetime. The press featured this presentation, and commentators labored to construe its meaning and significance.

A week after Acheson spoke in Mississippi, Winston Churchill, addressing a large audience in London's Albert Hall, described the woeful plight of almost all Europe and averred that only if its many countries worked together in close unity could they overcome their distress and be secure. With dramatic rhetoric he had asked the question: "What is Europe now?" and his answer was, "It is a rubble heap, a charnel house, a breeding ground of pestilence and hate." He called upon the British and other governments to seek a solution for their problems by means of attitudes and measures that were European, not narrowly national. This speech of Churchill's stirred the gusts of discussion about a coordinated program. By May 23d the report of the Policy Planning Staff was completed, and Kennan gave it to Marshall in the compressed form which the Secretary favored. As succinctly summed up by Eric F. Goldman, it recommended that the American Government should make "a massive offer of American resources, directed toward all of Europe with no ideological overtones, in a positive effort to restore the economy of the continent. There were two important provisions. The Europeans had to take the initiative in working out all details, and the program which the Europeans submitted had to give promise of doing the 'whole job. . . . [of · being] the last such program we shall be asked to support in the foreseeable future.' "

The program, Kennan's report to Marshall stressed, should be formulated and developed jointly by the European countries, not by us, and it should contemplate a coordinated effort, not to be merely a combination of separate and perhaps competitive national programs.

· · · · ·

The issue hardest to determine was whether our offer should be addressed to the whole of Europe, including the Soviet Union and its satellites, or merely to the more attached and democratic nations of western Europe.

Kennan feared that the Soviet Government would try either to link any proposal made to its own particular aims—such as the exaction of reparations from Germany or the administration of the Ruhr—or if it should accept, seek to make the whole plan fail. Nevertheless, he thought the Soviets should be given the chance to participate, while the American and other governments retained the right to decide whether the conditions of their participation were acceptable.

Eric Goldman has related, probably paraphrasing what he was told, a short dialogue between Marshall and Kennan.

Marshall: "Are we safe in directing such a proposal to all of Europe? What will be the effect if the Soviets decide to come in?"

Kennan: "What better way to emphasize that the program is not mere anti-Sovietism? Why not make the American proposition one which said to Russia, 'You, like ourselves, produce raw materials which Western Europe needs, and we shall be glad to examine together what contributions you as well as we could make.' This would mean that Russia would either have to decline or else agree to make a real contribution, herself, to the revival of the western European economy."

Acheson's and Clayton's thoughts concorded. Their reasoning, as delineated by Jones was: ". . . that it would be a colossal error for the United States to put itself in a position where it could be blamed for the division of Europe. The psychological and political advantage of asking all Europeans to get together would disappear if we should divide Europe by offering to help rebuild only half of it. The problem, however, was a very difficult one. If the Russians came in the whole project would probably be unworkable because the amount of money involved in restoring both Eastern and Western Europe would be so great it could never be got from Congress, especially in view of the strong and growing reaction against the Soviet Union. But there was a strong probability that the U.S.S.R. would never come in on a basis of disclosing full information about their economic and financial condition, which was necessary if a common recovery plan were to work."

Marshall decided to give the Russians the chance to contribute as well as to benefit, by providing raw materials in exchange for assistance. If they would not, the American Government should go ahead and let them exclude themselves.

The risk would be taken. But it was to be carefully safeguarded by the way in which Marshall's presentation was to be worded. It would call on each and any European participant to disclose its economic and financial situation, to define its needs, to subject its estimates of justified help to discussion, and to abide by the same principles and arrangements for mutual help as others.

The draft of the speech Marshall was going to make at the Harvard commencement exercises was completed during the first days of June. He rewrote the sentences defining the initiative which European countries were to be encouraged to take, and while flying to Cambridge again changed the language slightly.

During the maturation of the proposal the initiative was not, as far as is known, systematically discussed with President Truman. Marshall, after his return from Europe in late April, had reported to him on the worrisome situation left at the end of the abortive conference of the Foreign Ministers; and he and Acheson had told him briefly of the plans which the State Department was developing. The President had permitted Marshall and Acheson to determine their range and content and to decide the way in which they would be put forward publicly. So great was Marshall's assurance that he did not deem it necessary to clear the text of his Harvard speech with Truman; and so great was Truman's confidence in Marshall that he did not request him to do so.

On the afternoon of June 5th, Marshall read the speech, dryly, seldom looking up and at his audience. It sounded deceptively simple. "The United States should do whatever it is able to do to assist in the return of normal economic health in the world, without which there can be no political stability and no assured peace. Our policy is directed not against any country or doctrine but against hunger, poverty, desperation, and chaos. Its purpose should be the revival of a working economy in the world so as to permit the emergence of political and social conditions in which free institutions can exist. Such assistance, I am convinced, must not be on a piece-meal basis as various crises develop. Any assistance that this government may render in the future should provide a cure rather than a mere palliative. Any government that is willing to assist in the task of recovery will find full cooperation, I am sure, on the part of the United States Government. Any government which manoeuvers to block the recovery of other countries cannot expect help from us. Furthermore, governments, political parties, or groups which seek to perpetuate human misery in order to profit therefrom politically or otherwise will encounter the opposition of the United States."

Following this exposition of our purpose, phrased so as to be both a bid and a warning to the Soviet Union, he continued: "It is already evident that, before the United States Government can proceed much further in its efforts to alleviate the situation and help start the European world on its way to recovery, there must be some agreement among the countries of Europe as to the requirements of the situation and the part those countries themselves will take in order to give proper effect to whatever action might be undertaken by this government. It would be neither fitting nor efficacious for this government to undertake to draw up unilaterally a program designed to place Europe on its feet economically. That is the business of the Europeans. The initiative, I think, must come from Europe. The role of this country should consist of friendly aid in the drafting of a European program and of later support of such a program so far as it may be practical for us to do so. The program should be a joint one, agreed to by a number [of], if not all, European nations."

Acheson briefed a few American reporters before Marshall's proposal was released. Moreover, being unsure of the speed in which Marshall's address— being a Commencement address—would be transmitted abroad through official channels, he confided in several British press correspondents. He told them that it would be of unusual importance and major intent, and that it merited urgent attention. They had telephoned the text to their editors with the suggestion that it be passed on at once to Bevin, so on the evening of the same day that Marshall spoke in Cambridge Bevin read the speech in London.

Bevin rejected a suggestion made by Sir William Strang, the Permanent Undersecretary of the Foreign Office, that the Chargé d'Affaires of the British Embassy in Washington be instructed to inquire of Marshall what he had in mind as the nature of the most suitable response. According to Acheson, Bevin answered, "Bill, we know what he *said*. If I ask questions you'll get answers you don't want. Our problem is what we *do,* not what he *meant*." Bevin let Marshall know that the British Government would take the sort of initiative he commended. So did Bidault.

On June 17th Bevin flew to Paris for two days of talk with Bidault. The French Foreign Minister urged that Molotov be asked to join them. The French Government was insecure and worried about the internal situation; it needed the votes of those Socialist Deputies who favored cooperation with Moscow. Bevin was willing to ask the Soviet Government whether it would join in this preliminary consideration of the response to be made to Marshall. After Molotov expressed an interest, he was formally invited to join Bevin and Bidault in Paris for talks to begin on June 27th. Molotov accepted.

In advance of the meeting of these three Foreign Ministers, Clayton went to London. Accompanied by our Ambassador to London, Lewis Douglas, he talked over with Bevin and his colleagues the procedure for developing a program of recovery for Europe and the nature of the program. The Americans reaffirmed that it must be a joint program and visualized a joint effort. Their ideas were not fixed or precise. Clayton's thoughts still strove to keep to the fore his favorite remedies for all ills—the reduction of trade restrictions and the releasing of currencies from control. But the British consultants argued that his analysis of the situation was too simple, that these measures alone could not save Europe then and there and would have to be taken gradually as conditions improved. The Chancellor of the Exchequer was, in particular, not pleased by Clayton's presence or ideas. Dalton was fearful of the consequences of making sterling freely convertible, as Britain was pledged to do under the terms of the American loan. Granting the need for gradualness, the Americans insisted that the program must evidence the interdependence of the participants and call forth the advantages of cooperation. The formulations at this stage did not, could not, deal in detail with the problems of adjustment of the national recipients to a master program.

The three Foreign Ministers met in Paris at the end of June. Each day the British Foreign Office let the American Government know how their talks were going.

Bidault proposed they be guided by Marshall's statement that the countries of Europe should take the initiative and together reach a joint accord among themselves about the needs and the aims. In this program it would be expected that each would both help itself and the others. Molotov then suggested that the American Government be asked how much it would give. Bevin demurred. He stubbornly maintained that the context of Marshall's statement made it clear that before answering this question the American Government would want to know what constructive joint plan the European governments themselves were able to conceive. By doing their best to help themselves not only individually but as a group, they could, he stressed, limit to a minimum the amount of aid they must ask of the United States.

At the next session (June 28th) Molotov insinuated that the American Government was activated by a wish to enlarge exports in view of the economic crisis he saw approaching in the United States. Then he strongly objected to the procedure whereby the European countries in conference would draw up a general economic program to which American help would be adjunct. Rather he urged that each country should continue as before to decide for itself the best ways to improve its condition. France and Britain, he said, each had its economic plan as did the Soviet Union, whose successive five-year plans were being realized and would assure constant increase in Soviet prosperity. Let each country, therefore, draw up its own statement of what it needed in the way of American aid. In conference thereafter, the European countries could consider the national statements and draw up a list of their total requirements and ascertain the possibility of getting such help from the United States. The Bidault-Bevin proposals would inevitably, he alleged, bring unwarranted outside interference with their national affairs. Moreover, the needs of those countries that had fought Germany and been occupied should have prior considerations and be the first group invited to take part in the prospective program. He was aggrieved because it was contemplated that Germany would be associated with the program, on the basis of information to be provided by the commanders of the four zones.

To this version of the answer to be made to Marshall, the Soviet officials clung. Russia was proudly maintaining the outward semblance of strength, although its people were in sore need of almost everything—food, clothing, housing, which was appallingly short, tools, transport. Food was so scarce because of the drought in the summer of 1946 that the Soviet Government had been compelled to continue bread rationing and to change its plans so as to give agriculture priority over heavy industry. But a good harvest in 1947 was in prospect, and enough reserve remained to carry over under strict control. Russia was defying its own wants, concealing its own deficiencies, rather than allowing itself to appear dependent on the bounty of capitalist United States. The use of men, materials, and machines for armaments was cramping; the Soviet Government was keeping the fear of war alive, so that its people should work hard, though weary and bewildered.

Molotov grew more open in his accusations. On July 2d—the first day of their talks—he alleged that the British and French Governments were trying to use Marshall's proposal as a pretext to create a new organization which could interfere in the affairs of independent countries and direct their development. The possibility of any country's securing an American credit, he argued, would be dependent on its "docile" conduct toward this organization and its Director. As examples he said the suggested arrangement would enable them to bring pressure on Poland to produce more coal and retard the growth of other industries; on Czechoslovakia to increase its production of food and reduce its production of machines; or on Norway to give up plans to create a steel industry on the grounds that this would better suit certain foreign steel companies. In such ways a combined plan would be an invasion of the sovereignty of all and end their economic independence.

This appraisal ignored the fact that no country would be coerced to agree to features of the combined plan it thought unacceptable, or into joining in it. Each would be free to judge for itself whether the benefits obtained would not outweigh any adaptations required of it.

Behind Molotov's arguments could be detected unwillingness to subject the Russian economic situation and program to discussion. But beyond that the Soviet spokesmen were posing as the defenders—against the American imperialists—of any of Russia's satellites who might be tempted to join in order to get American help (Poland, Czechoslovakia, and Hungary were tempted). He warned Bevin and Bidault that the participants in the combined program being considered would be separated from other European countries. Europe would be divided; one group would be opposed against another. This, he said, might seem advantageous to certain great powers (the United States) who wanted to dominate others.

Milovan Djilas, an emissary of Tito's, was in Paris at the time. In his book *Conversations with Stalin,* he offers an explanation of why Molotov during the previous days had appeared to be considering some kind of compromise procedure. Djilas states that Molotov told him that the Soviet Government was going to refuse to join the conference which was being proposed and that he, Djilas, said Yugoslavia would also do so. But Molotov was turning over another tactic in his mind. He was wondering ". . . whether a conference should not be called in which the Eastern countries would also participate, but only for propaganda reasons, with the aim of exploiting the publicity and then walking out of the conference at a convenient moment. I was not enthusiastic about this variation either, though I would not have opposed it had the Russians insisted. . . . However, Molotov received a message from the Politburo in Moscow that he should not agree even to this." There are corroboratory accounts of the receipt of a message which agitated Molotov and instructed him to cease discussion of Russian participation.

There was in Molotov's demeanor and response, as there had been in so many of the Communist denunciations of the United States, a *jealous* rage. The U.S. could offer what the Soviet Union could not.

four
dean acheson and "situations of strength"

LLOYD C. GARDNER

Lloyd C. Gardner, professor of history at Rutgers
University, is a prominent representative of the New
Left school. Born in Delaware, Ohio, in 1934, Gardner
received his A.B. from Ohio Wesleyan University
and his M.A. and Ph.D. from the University of Wisconsin.
As a graduate student at Wisconsin, Gardner became a
part of the vanguard of young New Left historians
studying under William A. Williams. His publications
include Economic Aspects of New Deal Diplomacy
(1964) and The Origins of the Cold War (1970), to
which Arthur Schlesinger, Jr., and Hans
Morgenthau also contributed their views. In Architects of
Illusion, from which the following selection is taken,
Gardner criticizes the doctrinaire attitudes of the chief
formulators of American policy in the early Cold
War. Sharing Bernstein's interpretation that American
hostility contributed to the Cold War, Gardner examines
the outlook and influence of Dean Acheson as one of
the chief proponents of containment. Considered in the
context of Feis's account, were Acheson's views as
illusory as Gardner suggests? How does Gardner's
description of the situation in Greece and Turkey differ
from that provided by Feis? In what ways do Gardner and
Feis disagree on the purpose behind the Truman
Doctrine and the Marshall Plan?

Source: Lloyd C. Gardner, Architects of Illusion: Men and Ideas
in American Foreign Policy, 1941–1949 (Chicago: Quadrangle,
1970), pp. 202–30. Copyright © 1970 by Lloyd C. Gardner.
Reprinted by permission of the publisher.

44

"If people are unreasonable," wrote an anonymous British Puritan in
the seventeenth century, "then must the Prince bow for a time and bring
them to his purpose by some craft or by some holy pretense." Like those
seventeenth-century Puritans who suddenly found themselves in power
at the end of the English civil war—when all society around them seemed
imperiled—Dean Acheson's convictions about revolution and social order led
him to "bow for a time," and to use reasons of state, policy, or the "holy
pretense" to secure men to his high purpose. The real issue, wrote Louis Halle,
one of Acheson's associates in the State Department at the time of the Truman
Doctrine, was the balance of power: "As in 1917, as in 1941, it was still not
possible to tell the American people what the real issue was." Halle's effort
to put the Cold War into a "realistic" mold might do justice to Machiavelli,
but not to the convictions of Dean Acheson.

The son of a clergyman, Acheson came to intellectual maturity in the World
War I era. He proclaimed himself a Wilsonian "liberal." Like the President he
emulated, Acheson's "liberalism" was coldly rational and austere, built upon
the edifice of Anglo-Saxon legal precedent. Both Wilson and Acheson were
completely dependent upon this structure for their political thought, which told
them that their country must play the key role "in the realignment of power
which the crumbling of empires and emergence of new forces necessitated."

. . . . .

Acheson had Wilson's gift of being able to lift the struggle up out of the dust
and sweat of the arena into the realm of the spirit, where life became a
"pilgrimage from birth to death through a battleground between good and evil."
"The individual," Acheson once wrote, "makes the pilgrimage to choose what is
good and reject what is evil, to transcend appetites and achieve the aspirations
of the spirit." Yet, as he pointed out on another occasion, the many facets of a
problem that confronted the policy-maker seldom could "be separated in the
intellectual equivalent of a cream separator." In August 1946 he told the
Associated Harvard Clubs in Boston that the continued moral, military, and
economic power of the United States was essential to organizing the peace and
to hastening recovery in other countries "along lines which are essential to our
own system." Acheson put all these ideas together during testimony on the bill to
aid Greece and Turkey. "What the President was talking about," he began,

and I think what we are trying to do in one part of the world by his bill,
is to assist people to live the kind of life and have the kind of
institutions which they wish to have. We are talking particularly about
free institutions, countries which have that system, a system in which we
believe. In this particular case they are under pressure which may force
them to give that up. And in that situation they ask for our help. We
are willing to help people who believe the way we do, to continue to
live the way they want to live.

By the time of the Korean War, Acheson was blaming the "distant and
shadowy figures in the Kremlin" for practically everything that had gone wrong

since World War II. Frustration and intense bitterness were natural in this struggle against evil, he wrote to a man whose son was stationed in Korea:

This agony of spirit, so understandable and right, makes it hard to believe that so monstrous an evil can exist in a world based upon infinite mercy and justice.
  But the fact is that it does exist. The fact is that it twists and tortures all our lives. And, I believe, to each of us in this case, as in so many others, the great thing is not what happens to us but how we bear what happens to us.

Upon this rock Acheson built a final justification for the American Cold War position. "It has been hard for us to convince ourselves that human nature is not pretty much the same the world over," he told the Advertising Council in 1950. "The only way to deal with the Soviet Union, we have found from hard experience, is to create situations of strength." There was very little to discuss with the Soviets when their very existence twisted and tortured "all our lives." As Acheson said in 1957, "It is my conviction that the only agreements which are possible now would be disadvantageous to us and would not diminish the dangers of nuclear war." Whatever way the so-called balance of power leaned after 1947, Acheson's views remained firm and unchanging through the Cold War, "peaceful coexistence," the Cuban missile crisis, and "realist" revisionism of the origins of the Cold War.

In Cold War histories, the Truman Doctrine speech of March 12, 1947, is generally regarded as the main turning point, though there is a great difference of opinion about how the signposts at that juncture should be read. Truman gave his own opinions on that matter in a special interview with members of the American Society of Newspaper Editors, shortly after he had gone before Congress to ask for substantial economic and military aid for Greece and Turkey. "There has been a great deal of speculation," he began, "as to the why and wherefore, and how it came about—to quote one paper that I saw, 'so suddenly.' It didn't come about so suddenly. . . . Back about the 25th of April, if I remember correctly, in 1945," Truman continued, Foreign Minister Molotov had called at the White House before going on to the United Nations organization conference. "He stated categorically what he expected to get out of San Francisco. And I told him, categorically, what he was going to get. And he made the statement when he went out of here that he had never been talked to in that manner by anybody before in his life. It did him good."
  After summarizing world events in the time between Molotov's visit and his own recent message, Truman concluded briskly:

And finally, when Great Britain came to the point where she could no longer maintain the situation in Greece and Turkey, I called in the Foreign Relations Committee of the House and the Senate, and the leaders of both parties in the House and the Senate, and laid the facts before them. . . . And that is how the situation developed. It wasn't a

*sudden proposition that happened in 5 minutes. It had been developing
ever since the Germans surrendered. And it finally got to the point
where we had to state our case to the world.*

Truman's recitation failed to note Dean Acheson's singular performance
during that White House conference with congressional leaders, though the
President later gave Acheson full credit for his achievements as Secretary
of State. "History I am sure," he wrote in his *Memoirs,* "will list Dean Acheson
among the truly great Secretaries of State our nation has had." Endowed, as
Truman said, with a "keen mind, cool temper, and broad vision," the Under
Secretary (at the time of the Greek crisis) was indeed a master logician, who,
once his premise was granted, could run circles around an adversary. If the
premise of a total Bolshevik challenge to Western civilization was not
self-evident in 1947, Acheson's vivid analyses at the White House meeting
preceding the Truman Doctrine Message, and his brilliant performances before
congressional committees in the weeks that followed, very nearly established the
threat permanently. His exposition of the "Mr. X" theme before the House
Foreign Affairs Committee in 1948 was a fine example of all these abilities. "I
think two things must be clear," Acheson began,

*to those who have considered Soviet policy over the past three decades.
The first is that the Soviet Union accepts with complete realism a strong
and stable situation and adjusts its policy accordingly. The other is that
the Soviet Union, with equal realism, accepts the opportunities offered
by weak and unstable situations whether they result from defeat and
occupation or from the exhaustion of an ally. It was the weakness of
Iran and Greece which led to pressure upon those countries. It was the
crisis of western Europe which led to internal Communist pressure in
Italy and France, where the Communist parties attempted to capitalize
on the difficulties of the people in an effort to overthrow the
governments. Such efforts will continue until there is internal stability.*

Having made the different Iranian and Greek situations quite indistinguishable
by invoking the "containment" theme, Acheson could develop that theme into
a complete theory of the current troubles in Western Europe: "This leads to
weakness and continual change of governments, unemployment, and the break-up
of employer-employee relations, the collapse of the financial system, and the
immediate disappearance of that large middle class upon which has been founded
the stability of western Europe."
Long before the Truman Doctrine speech in 1947, these views had
consolidated into Acheson's world outlook. The change that came over the Under
Secretary following that speech consisted first in putting together the total nature
of the challenge—primarily the link-up of the Soviet Union and world
revolution—then in making use of the holy pretense to combat it. Once put
together properly, this new view held sway without further conscious effort. The
essential fact of the European situation, Acheson advised the House Foreign
Affairs Committee in 1948, was that those nations could not have sound internal

economic systems without large-scale foreign trade. Shut off from Eastern European trade, they would have to look elsewhere to maintain their present social and economic organization, especially to Southeast Asia where, under the stimulus of the Marshall Plan, it was to be hoped a large part of Europe's exports would go. Otherwise European nations would suffer internal revolutions from which minority governments would emerge and turn inevitably to the only alternative: "the closed economic system which now extends from Poland to the Pacific." "The Communist area cannot solve the problem," Acheson concluded, "but it can promise some amelioration of it. The result may well be, as it has already been with some of the countries of eastern Europe, the inclusion of still further areas within the Russian system and the extension of Russian domination still further westward."

Acheson had developed a double-domino theory: Russia pushed outward until confronted with sufficient force to halt the progression of dominoes falling westward, while the Western countries themselves had to be held up so that they would not fall to the east. By this somewhat confusing metaphor, it was possible to convince a Congressman that almost any result would follow logically. The Greek case is a good example: In 1947 Acheson admitted to one congressional committee that "many persons" honestly supported the "communist-led" forces opposing the present Greek government. A year later such distinctions were unnecessary. "The [Greek] civil war was *instigated* and aided by people from the outside," Acheson affirmed uncritically, then promptly agreed with a demonstrably erroneous statement from a committee member that less than 1 per cent of the people supported the attacks upon the government in Athens.

Although there had been no specific outside military threat to Greece in 1947, such statements, by making it seem there had indeed been a serious threat, prepared the people for the next step in the Cold War. The whole process amounted to almost total disregard for the realities of the situation. However, Russian probes in the Mediterranean since 1945 did help Acheson to make his presentation of Greek turmoil look like a total crumbling of defenses before the barbarian onslaught from the East. Churchill, who had first offered that interpretation of Greek events, used the Truman Doctrine message to chide his American critics in a letter to the editor of the *New York Times*: "On Greek affairs in 1944–45 I seemed to find myself out of step. But today it seems I was pursuing the exact policy which, little more than two years later, the United States has adopted with strong conviction. This is to me a very intense satisfaction." If no longer so simplistic in Acheson's explications, Churchill's defense was still basically self-serving for both Great Britain and the United States, albeit for somewhat different reasons.

The Greek struggle against British imperialism appealed to Americans in 1944–1945, but only when the Cold War developed did they support— ironically—the "imperialists." Although Roosevelt had never really accepted the arrangement as final, Greece had been assigned to Great Britain during the 1944 Churchill-Stalin discussion of the Balkans. Turkey had not been discussed that day, but the heart of the "Eastern Question" had always been control of the Dardanelles. From March 1947 on, the United States became responsible for "containing" Russian expansion in this area. To stop there, however, is to put much too negative a connotation on American policy in the Eastern Mediterranean after World War II. Truman's repeated efforts to push American influence into the Danube area, as well as to secure an "open-door" regime in the Turkish Straits, provided the frustrated President with more than enough evidence on which to base a new doctrine. American interest in securing equal access to other Middle Eastern countries went back much earlier than the London Foreign Ministers' Conference or Potsdam. John C. Campbell's able review of *The United States in World Affairs, 1945–1947,* generalized this theme aptly:

We wished to develop the Middle East's resources and to increase our trade in friendly competition with Great Britain, loosening if we could the ties of the sterling bloc. Some called it a policy of "underwriting the British Empire." But that empire was itself in the process of drastic change and partial liquidation. There were signs that, by force of events, American policy might be developed along the more imaginative lines suggested by Dean [James] Landis as "a substitute for empire under the superstructure of San Francisco." The result would be about the same. Both the United States and Great Britain favored the organization of the Near and Middle East within the "western" political and economic orbit, without denying independence to its peoples. They wished to strengthen its weak spots and particularly to hold up Soviet expansion on its northern rim, in Turkey and Iran.

Since the first decade of the twentieth century, Great Britain and Russia had divided Iran between them. While American economic and political interest in the country had also blossomed, it did not get the chance to crack this diumvirate until 1942 when American troops moved into the country to insure that the Persian Gulf supply route to the Soviet Union remained open. In 1943 American diplomats slipped into Iranian economics and politics via this military route; then the United States took a big leap forward into Iranian affairs by insisting upon the Teheran Declaration in 1943. The declaration pledged the Big Three to respect Iranian political and economic independence after the war.

One of the State Department's special advisers to the Shah's government was Arthur C. Millspaugh, who developed (at Roosevelt's specific request) an expansive program for implementing the Teheran Declaration by a twenty-year economic aid program—a New Deal for Iran. While Roosevelt was "rather thrilled with the idea of using Iran as an example of what we could do by an unselfish American policy," he quickly concluded it was a task for younger men. One younger man in the State Department, Herbert Hoover, Jr., picked up the task and turned it over to an American oil company seeking a large concession in Iran; Hoover thus restored the initiative to private enterprise, a move faithful to his father's tradition. Millspaugh, himself deeply interested in expanding American interests, was shocked at the way this matter was handled: "It is surprising that our government should have launched such a combustible enterprise in an unstable area in the midst of war. It is equally surprising that in view of our devotion to three-power cooperation and to the principle of equal access to raw materials we should have applied for the concession with no understanding with the Soviet Union and none of any practical value, unless we had a secret one, with Great Britain."

The ruling Shah was especially pleased at this evidence of long-term American interest in his country while it was still occupied by British and Soviet troops. When, however, these latter powers demanded a share in any new oil concessions, he was not so well satisfied. His Ambassador told the State Department that the Shah had responded by postponing all talk of concessions until after the war, when foreign troops had been removed according to the Declaration on Iran. "Iran should be of special interest to Americans after the war," added the Ambassador. "All other countries in that part of the world were affiliated with British or French interests, while Iran was free of such affiliations, and his country was furthermore in an important position *as a back door to Russia.*"

When they learned about the American oil policy, the Soviets had demanded a concession over most of northern Iran, and protested the Shah's decision to postpone talks both in Teheran and in Washington. . . .

Although excluded from Anglo-American oil diplomacy in the Middle East, the Russians had far more than a simple economic interest in Iran. Thus they responded to the Anglo-American policy with an effort to detach Azerbaijan from Iran and turn it into a satellite. Yet what is often forgotten about this struggle is that it took place in the midst of a general American movement into the Middle East, one which brooked no opposition from the Soviets, Britain, or France. . . .

The situation in Iran, meanwhile, had become acute by the fall of 1945, when the Shah's army tried to reoccupy provinces evacuated by the Soviets, who were now cheering on local communists in Azerbaijan. Byrnes and Bevin both pressed Stalin on this question at the Moscow Foreign Ministers' Conference. In reply, Russian leaders charged that American and British troops had not withdrawn from Greece and Indonesia, alleged that the Iranian government was unfriendly to the Soviet Union, and finally insisted that it was necessary to protect the nearby Baku oil fields from saboteurs. . . .

On January 19, 1946, the Iranian delegate to the London meeting of the General Assembly formally complained of Russian interference in the internal affairs of his country. After several days of debate the Security Council called upon the Soviet Union and Iran to settle the matter by direct negotiations between them. Meanwhile, in Teheran the Big Three ambassadors paid a visit to Premier Ghavam-es-Sultaneh to give him "friendly advice" on how to handle the situation.

The negotiations failed, however, and in March the question was back before the United Nations. In new bilateral negotiations the Russians pledged to remove their troops in five to six weeks. But the terms they agreed to were not exactly what Washington had hoped for in encouraging the Iranians to bring the question before the U.N. The Soviets demanded the creation of a joint Russian-Iranian oil company to exploit potential resources in the northern provinces, and assurances of a good deal of local autonomy for Azerbaijan. . . .

After the Russians finally evacuated northern Iran, American influence in the

Iranian parliament blocked the ratification of the Russian oil concession, and American advisers were at the head of the troops the Shah sent into Azerbaijan.

Far from justifying the Truman Doctrine, the Iranian episode revealed that it was possible to extend American interests even to the doorstep of the Soviet Union without effective challenge. "The U.S.S.R.'s recognition of this fact," said *Business Week,* "accounts for Moscow's aggressive diplomacy in northern Iran, for the bitter Soviet demands that British troops get out of Greece, and for feverish Russian diplomatic activity in Egypt, Syria, Iraq and Iran." By 1953 America also had almost completely replaced British influence in Iran, and had a 40 per cent cut of the old Anglo-Iranian oil holdings.

What then of the supposed strategic threat to the Dardanelles?

.   .   .   .   .

Moscow repeated its original demands for joint control in a long note to the Turks on August 7, 1946. At that point, Acting Secretary of State Dean Acheson took his first serious initiative in Middle Eastern affairs, calling a meeting of the State-War-Navy Coordinating Committee and the Joint Chiefs of Staff to consider the serious situation created by the Russian note. He opened the meeting by emphasizing the gravity of the matter. It was clear, so far as he was concerned, that the Russians were trying to take over the straits and would eventually establish naval and air beachheads there if they succeeded. The problem, then, was whether the United States could—or would—stand with the Turks to defend the gates into the Mediterranean.

If so, a note should be sent to the Russians, gentle in tone but absolutely firm in purpose. There was general agreement around the table that the Acting Secretary's proposal was the only way to meet the threat. Several days after this secret meeting, James Reston wrote in the *New York Times* that Acheson was in fact developing "a foreign policy," one which would demonstrate to Moscow that the United States did not intend to repeat the political mistakes it had made after World War I. Acheson was convinced, Reston said, that the emerging disputes called for a long-term commitment to internationalism. The Acting Secretary was "aware of the dangers involved in the policy of intervention . . . but [felt] that the dangers of intervention [were] less than the dangers of non-intervention."

Put in the context of Russia's withdrawal from Iran, its abandonment of prior claims to trustee rights over a former Italian colony in Africa, and other signs of retreat in the Mediterranean, Reston's analysis deserves serious attention as an alternate way of explaining the foreign policy then being developed by the Acting Secretary of State. It was indeed based on a long-term commitment to internationalism and intervention. The State Department's August 19 note to Moscow warned that any attack on the straits by an aggressor would justify the Security Council in taking action. Truman backed up the message by sending the aircraft carrier *Franklin D. Roosevelt,* four cruisers, and a destroyer flotilla to the eastern Mediterranean to join the battleship *Missouri,* stationed there since April. Navy Secretary Forrestal announced that these vessels would be placed on permanent station in the Mediterranean—the first such act since Jefferson's day. Ankara promptly rejected the Soviet proposal, and once again the Russian threat melted away.

Dean Acheson's August 19 note was potentially embarrassing to the State Department, should any later critic of the Truman Doctrine have brought it up at those congressional hearings. It was made public in the State Department *Bulletin* at the time, but later ignored. The note read: "It is observed that the note of the Soviet Government contains no reference to the United Nations. The position of the Government of the United States is that the regime of the Straits should be brought into appropriate relationship with the United Nations and should function in a manner entirely consistent with the principles and aims of the United Nations." But in 1947 the administration paid no heed to its own advice that the U.N. should underwrite Big Three policies. Instead it pushed forward with unilateral military aid, justifying it in ways that actually weakened the U.N.

The increasingly obsolete mainstay of Western influence was still British military and economic aid, but this finally gave way on Friday afternoon, February 21, 1947, when the British Embassy asked for an appointment with Secretary of State Marshall. The Secretary had left his office, so it was decided to postpone the meeting until Monday. In the meantime, the First Secretary might bring over the documents so that preparations could be made over the weekend. Later that afternoon, therefore, the British handed two notes to Loy Henderson, director of the Office of Near Eastern Affairs. In Greece, said the first note, the economic situation was near collapse. That country needed between $240 and $280 million in financial aid in the next few months. London would be unable to offer further assistance after March 31. The second note on Turkey simply stated that Britain could not underwrite the modernization of the Turkish army. "Reading the messages," Henderson and his associates realized "that Great Britain had within the hour handed the job of world leadership, with all its burdens and all its glory, to the United States."

The following Thursday, Marshall and Acheson met with congressional leaders in the White House. The conference did not begin well:

Things were going very badly indeed, and Acheson was greatly disturbed. Leaning over to Secretary Marshall, who sat beside him, Acheson asked in a low voice, "Is this a private fight or can anyone get into it?" Whereupon Marshall addressed the President and suggested that Acheson had something to say.

For the next ten to fifteen minutes the Under Secretary spoke as a fervent advocate of the American mission in a suddenly bipolarized world, a last Athens or Rome against the greatest and most dangerous Sparta or Carthage. The defense of Western civilization, even the sacred place of its birth, had been left up to the United States. In a world where one of the two great powers was aggressive and expanding, the protection of countries threatened by Soviet aggression *or* communist subversion was not pulling chestnuts out of the fire for anyone—it was the protection of freedom itself. Once the Russians succeeded in gaining control of the eastern Mediterranean, the possibilities for further penetration into Asia and Africa became almost limitless. And in Western Europe the psychological impact on countries like Italy and France, with their large communist minorities, would be devastating, if not conclusive.

"When [Acheson] finished," an aide noted, "a profound silence ensued that lasted perhaps ten seconds." It was broken by Senator Vandenberg, who said he had been greatly impressed, even shaken by what he had heard. But, he added, if the President wanted to get any results, he would have to "scare hell out of the country." Leaving the White House, Acheson held an off-the-record press conference with correspondents who regularly covered the State Department. Giving them the sense of the British notes, he carefully explained the situation in the same terms he had used hours earlier. The first "scare" had been well placed. The next day formal work began on details of the program to be recommended to Congress and the President's speech which would sound the tocsin.

Joseph M. Jones was assigned the task of drafting the original working paper for the President's message. A few days earlier, he had himself previewed the British notes, and what they would imply for the United States, in a letter to Senator William Benton:

There are many signs that the world is approaching this year the greatest crisis since the turn in the tide of the war in November, 1942. It is primarily an economic crisis centered in Britain and Empire, France, Greece and China. . . . If these areas are allowed to spiral downwards into economic anarchy, then at best they will drop out of the United States orbit and try an independent nationalistic policy; at worst they will swing into the Russian orbit. We will then face the world alone. What will be the cost in dollars and cents of our armaments and of our economic isolation? I do not see how we could possibly avoid a depression far greater than that of 1929–1932 and crushing taxes to pay for the direct commitments we would be forced to make around the world.

In the *New York Times* of March 2, 1947, Hanson Baldwin sounded a more ideological theme taken directly from Acheson's briefings. The United States, Baldwin said, "far more than any single factor, is the key to the destiny of tomorrow; we alone may be able to avert the decline of Western civilization, and a reversion to nihilism and the Dark Ages."

A week before the President went before Congress, he spoke on foreign economic policy at Baylor University. His remarks began with the statement that world peace and freedom were all bound up in the problem of reestablishing world trade. The three goals were inseparable: "The grave lessons of the past have proved it. . . . We are the giant of the economic world. Whether we like it or not, the future pattern of economic relations depends upon us. The world is waiting and watching to see what we shall do. The choice is ours. We can lead the nations to economic peace or we can plunge them into economic war."

There was one thing, the President continued, that Americans valued more than peace:

*It is freedom. Freedom of worship—freedom of speech—freedom
of enterprise. . . . Throughout history, freedom of worship and
freedom of speech have been most frequently enjoyed in those
societies that have accorded a considerable measure of freedom
to individual enterprise. . . . So our devotion to freedom of
enterprise, in the United States, has deeper roots than a desire
to protect the profits of ownership.* It is part and parcel of what we
call American.

The trade pattern least conducive to freedom of enterprise was the one
in which decisions were made solely or principally by governments. ". . . If
this trend is not reversed, the Government of the United States will be under
pressure . . . to fight for markets and raw materials. And if the Government
were to yield to this pressure, it would shortly find itself in the business
of allocating foreign goods among importers and foreign markets among
exporters, and telling every trader what he could buy or sell. . . . It is not
the American way."

Truman's White House advisers wanted to continue the Baylor themes in
the message on Greece and Turkey. "If, by default," one draft stated,
"we permit free enterprise to disappear in the other nations of the world,
the very existence of our own economy and our own democracy will be
threatened." Acheson raised objections to all such specifics. He had been
insisting that the matter ought to be phrased in general and ideological
terms—totalitarianism versus freedom. Acheson therefore deleted another
White House reference to American interest in the natural resources of the
Middle East. Truman later put it in his memoirs, speaking of Russia's
threat to Iran as one which endangered Western economies and the "raw
material balance of the world." Acheson explained to Clark Clifford that even
the reference to the trend away from free enterprise would adversely affect
current relations with Great Britain, and give certain elements who were
upset by the British loan another shot at the administration.

Truman's message drew hard and fast ideological lines around the world.
By constant references to free and unfree peoples, democratic and totalitarian
governments, the President led Congress to his key paragraph: "I believe
that it must [Truman had changed the State Department's "should" to
"must"] be the policy of the United States to support free peoples who are
resisting attempted subjugation by armed minorities or by outside pressure."
Elsewhere in the speech Truman referred to the United Nations, but in
such a way as to make it clear the United States had assumed the burden of
defining how the status quo might be changed: "The world is not static, and
the status quo is not sacred. But we cannot allow changes in the status quo in
violation of the Charter of the United Nations by such methods as coercion, or
by such subterfuges as political infiltration. In helping free and independent
nations to maintain their freedom, the United States will be giving effect
to the principles of the Charter of the United Nations."

Even friends of the administration were troubled by the speech and the answers they received to their questionings. Overt Soviet military moves in the Mediterranean had virtually come to an end, yet the Truman Doctrine sounded a call to arms. "It was something like the feeling on the day of Munich," said Paul Smith, the *San Francisco Chronicle*'s editor and a close friend of Secretary Forrestal. "The man in the street began thinking about the taste of brackish water in canteens, and the mud of foxholes, and the smell of the dead, and all those reminders of the recently finished war, and wondering . . ." In answer to Smith's editorials and private questions, Forrestal answered that America had to keep the Mediterranean a free highway for "this economy of ours. . . . These raw materials have to come over the sea and a good many have to go through the Mediterranean." Although Smith eventually supported the Greek-Turkish aid bill, his concern about the way Truman pictured the struggle was shared by a good many others. In his newspaper he warned the administration that some would want to build the Truman Doctrine higher and higher around Russia until it was "so stifling that war would explode inevitably as the one means of breaking the stranglehold. That eventuality . . . is one of the alternative avenues down which the new policy could lead us."

Another newsman, Howard K. Smith, was in Moscow covering the Foreign Ministers' Conference of March–April 1947. As a direct result of the President's dramatic appearance before Congress, he wrote, the whole atmosphere changed, not only in Moscow itself but all through Eastern Europe, where the last representatives of non-Communist parties were soon driven from the governments of Hungary and Bulgaria. . . .

Acheson's policy of building "situations of strength" began with the Truman Doctrine and continued into the next decade with the Korean War. He knew full well that such a quest was unlikely ever to produce a clear military advantage over the Soviet Union. He had said as much in his September 1945 memorandum to Truman on atomic energy. In 1949, however, he became a vigorous advocate of the hydrogen bomb on the grounds that not developing it would lead to an "erosion" of American power and force negotiations between East and West on unfavorable terms. The search for a perfect negotiating position is, of course, the most unreal of all diplomatic postures—and the most suitable to the holy pretense. With the Truman Doctrine the United States had declared to the world that it would decide when changes in the status quo violated the U.N. Charter, when revolutions were strictly an internal affair, and when they were fomented from abroad by coercion, subterfuge, or political infiltration.

"It is not unfair to Acheson," wrote political scientist Coral Bell in *Negotiation from Strength* (1963), "to see in his attitude . . . a hint of the free-thinking clergyman, with his own reservations about the pearly gates, feeling it psychologically proper nevertheless to inspire the Sunday-school class to virtue with the prospect of ultimate bliss crowning a period of meritorious endeavour." Whether as puritan divine or free-thinking clergyman, Acheson's Sunday school was the Congress of the United States, which held yet a few backsliders. Moreover, General Eisenhower had recently made a statement to thirty-five members of Congress that Greece and Turkey were not of strategic importance to the United States, and could not be held in time of crisis.

Support to Greece thus posed a particularly difficult problem when Acheson appeared before the House Committee to defend Truman's request. Representative Jacob Javits suggested that there ought to be some way to exact commitments from Athens for serious political reforms. Acheson insisted first that the 1946 Greek election had been a fair one, then explained that the United States was not helping any specific party to maintain power. It only sought to aid a duly elected government operating under a legitimate constitution. Javits suspected that the Greek constitution was about as effective under the party in power as the American Constitution had been under the Bourbon redeemers in Mississippi. Acheson's concern for constitutional processes was supported by a dark vision of the alternative:

Those people will continue to be there until constitutionally they are removed. If we allow Greece to go to pieces, then you are quite right, you probably will have a commissar in charge of the place in short order.

Javits resented Acheson's attempts to set aside his original question by "scare" tactics, and he remonstrated politely, but quite forcefully, that the Under Secretary was not answering his question:

Mr. Secretary, is not that explanation just a little bit—and I am not using this term invidiously at all—but just to get us clear, is it not a little pat, because we know very well that not less than 20 percent of the people in Greece failed to participate in the last election on political grounds.

Nor would Javits concede the administration's argument that the partisans were inspired and directed from Bulgaria and Yugoslavia. Shouldn't we consider a new election as one of the key ways to pacify the country? he asked. Acheson's reply was too nicely diplomatic to suit Javits and other dissenters, especially at a hearing where administration witnesses had been imploring Congress to accept full political responsibility for an area previously dominated by European nations: "Whether or not any advisers we would have there would advise the Greek Government to hold elections, I cannot possibly say."

Javits simply refused to be put off. Had the Greek government been "advised" to offer the rebels amnesty, he queried? That had been done, said the Under Secretary, "and it has been offered."

"But it has not been coupled with any prospect of a new election?" Javits continued. No, Acheson said, "and I see no particular reason why it should be."

"Realistically, is it not a fact, Mr. Secretary, what we ask the Greek Government to do will go a very long way toward getting them to do it, especially under these circumstances?"

"I should think our advice would be taken seriously, yes."

"To say the least . . ."

So the exchange ended, without satisfying Javits on any count. As for the Turkish government, the administration made no serious attempt to picture it as democratic; and it was quite evident in the hearings that, as one witness put it, when "the new dish was being prepared for American consumption, Turkey was slipped into the oven with Greece because that seemed to be the surest way to cook a tough bird."

But Representative Helen Gahagan Douglas asked Acheson why the United States had not insisted that Turkey take its complaint directly to the U.N., instead of appealing for American military aid against Soviet encroachments. The Under Secretary replied a bit patronizingly: "My judgment would be that that would not be a productive course." Even so, said Mrs. Douglas, "we would have gained much. . . . We could then act on the unilateral plan that we now have under consideration, but we would have first explored the possibility of settling the problem through the international machinery which we helped set up. If we do not do so are we not culpable morally before the world?"

Acheson's reply was a study in holy hair-splitting: "I should not say so. I really think we ought not to use this word 'unilateral' quite as freely as some of us do. Unilateral means something that one country does. What we are now talking about here is responding to a request of another country. That at least involves two countries."

Conservative Senator Harry Byrd was not convinced. On April 22 on the floor of the Senate he charged that after sixteen days had elapsed, and after Congress had been called upon to provide the funds for the Greek-Turkish problem, our representative to the world organization had done nothing more than give notice to that body of American intentions. Byrd roundly lambasted the Russians for the next several minutes, but finally called for a showdown on these issues within the United Nations. In conclusion he raised two key questions: "If our unilateral action in arming other nations is provocative of war, upon what ally can we depend? If we act independently and arm nations to oppose communism, can we assume that Russia will not follow our lead and establish a counterpolicy?"

Such charges were serious enough to force bipartisan leaders to attempt to plaster over the "colossal blunder," as Senator Vandenberg called it, of ignoring the United Nations. He offered an amendment to the bill which provided that when the U.N. felt capable of taking over the work in Greece and Turkey, or of terminating it, the United States would accept a majority vote to that effect in either the Security Council or the General Assembly. Subtle as his mind was, Acheson had not thought of that one. A Russian veto could have blocked an attempt to initiate action in the U.N., but Vandenberg's amendment would have also made it impossible for the Soviets to step in after the plan was going full steam. And it looked good to the American public as well.

The bill called for $400 million to Greece and Turkey. Sixty-two per cent of the money was designated for military aid. This was the main reason why the program could not be sold through the United Nations in the first place. "I was shocked at the impression given by the President and by Assistant Secretary of State [Willard] Thorp, and by Mr. [Henry] Villard," said an anti-administration witness, left-liberal economist Broadus Mitchell, "that this was primarily to go for feeding people. The hunger, the illness, in Greece particularly, was dwelt upon—the need for restoring the economy of that wartorn country. Then, we are told by Assistant Secretary of State Clayton, in charge of economic affairs, of all people, that almost two-thirds of the amount of $400,000,000 is to go for war purposes."

Approval of the Greek-Turkish aid plan by Congress, even after all these questionings and revelations, significantly reduced congressional control of foreign affairs. Through a blend of puritan dogma and Yankee pragmatism, Americans justified even their own self-deception in the cause of anti-communism. In this atmosphere liberalism became almost pure relativism, conservatism chauvinism: Joseph Alsop soon sounded like Fulton Lewis, and vice versa.

Having scared hell out of the American people, and a good many Western European leaders as well, the administration tried to channel its response to the Soviet threat into more positive directions. The militance had been necessary, argued some who justified Truman's speech, in order to call attention to the seriousness of the threat. Acheson had already initiated studies which ultimately led to the Marshall Plan for European economic recovery. He then explained why it was necessary to enlist the support of all special interest groups in Congress behind the Marshall Plan.

"We had at that time a tremendous export surplus," Acheson recalled for Jonathan Daniels on one occasion, "as we still do, but there was then very little likelihood of the recipient nations being able to fill the dollar gap. It was also clear that if our exports did not continue, the political consequences in the battle of resistance against the spread of Communism in Europe would be lost." But should the United States fail to meet this challenge, Secretary Marshall said, there would inevitably be other consequences for the nation. "It would impose incalculable burdens upon this country and force serious readjustments in our traditional way of life. One of our important freedoms—freedom of choice in both domestic and foreign affairs—would be drastically curtailed."

Marshall's speech at Harvard on June 5, 1947, offered European leaders significant American economic aid if they would work together to restore the institutions of the old order on an inter-European basis. But they had to come up with a plan which would promise substantial recovery within a reasonable number of years, yet stay within a cost figure which Congress would approve. Several officers in the State Department besides Under Secretary Acheson had contributed to the speech, but George Frost Kennan supplied the answer to the $64 Question: What about the Soviet Union?

Marshall was naturally concerned that if Eastern Europe and the Soviet Union were invited to participate, Congress would then refuse to supply the necessary money. On the other hand, if these nations were automatically excluded at the start, how would the rest of Europe react? Kennan's advice was to "play it straight." He had opposed the Truman Doctrine speech, and in fact had opposed any aid to Turkey as an unnecessary risk. When asked about the Marshall Plan, he was even more emphatic that the United States should not define the area that would receive American aid. Following the Marxist maxim, "From each according to his ability, to each according to his need," Kennan remarked, the Russians could be invited to share in the burdens as well as the benefits of a common recovery program. One could almost be certain that the Russians would refuse, for this would force them to forgo a chance to exploit Western weaknesses.

In proposing this plan, American leaders were aware, then, that it would complete the division of Europe, whether or not the initiative belonged to the United States. But if Greece and Turkey "and the other countries should adopt closed economies," Will Clayton warned Congress, "you can imagine the effect that it would have on our foreign trade . . . it is important that we do everything we can to retain those export markets." The deterioration of the European economy would force those countries to adopt state controls, Acheson told another House committee in 1948. Their domestic economies would then have to be severely regulated, and ultimately the American system of free enterprise would be endangered.

In this view the specific moved quickly to the general: the Truman Doctrine became the Marshall Plan, the Anglo-American loan agreement became a general effort to stabilize currencies in all Europe. The eagerness with which the British Labour government reached for American aid and encouraged the French to do the same demonstrated that the 1946 loan had served its political purpose: it had "contained" British socialism, even if it had not met an immediate economic success.

Acting upon Marshall's suggestion, British and French leaders constituted themselves into a "steering committee" and called a preliminary conference for Paris. They were chagrined when Moscow not only accepted an invitation to attend the meetings but sent eighty-nine experts with Foreign Minister Molotov. Bevin and Bidault glowered at the Russians through six days of acrimonious debate over Molotov's proposal that each nation prepare a shopping list, a proposal which cut directly against Marshall's warning that any plan should provide for an overall European balance sheet. When no one wanted to compromise, Molotov shooed his eighty-nine assistants back to the Paris airport and departed, hurling charges that the American plan would subvert Europe's national economies—a fine ironic prophecy from a Bolshevik commissar to Europe's capitalist leaders.

But Molotov had had a second reason for attending the Paris meeting: Russian concern over the German question. The Truman Doctrine had been announced just as the Moscow Conference of Foreign Ministers began discussions of that question. Since it had forestalled serious consideration of the problem there, the Kremlin had seen the Paris meeting as an opportunity to press the Big Three. Throughout the six days he was in Paris, Molotov insisted that Germany could be considered only by the Foreign Ministers. Proposals at Paris to study the ways German resources might be integrated into the European recovery project, Molotov charged, ignored prior reparations claims by those countries which had suffered from German aggression. These remained unsatisfied, he said, and yet it was now proposed to use German resources for quite different purposes.

After the Russians left, the presence of Czech and Polish representatives at Paris soon proved embarrassing to both sides. The Czechs had even agreed to attend a second conference sometime in the future to work out details of the economic plan. This desire for Western aid was widely hailed by Anglo-French sources as a break with Moscow. Two days later, however, Foreign Minister Jan Masaryk announced that Prague had reversed its position. Both Washington and Moscow made sure that other grey areas between East and West disappeared. Throughout June and July, for example, the State Department agitated the Eastern European question regularly in its *Bulletin*. Coalition cabinets in France and Italy were reorganized in May and June, excluding the left parties, especially any Communist ministers.

In Prague during the summer of 1947, Czech leaders were trapped between American rhetoric and foreign bayonets. James Warburg personally witnessed their agony with a sense of foreboding about the future that grew day by day. Conversations with Jan Masaryk and the American Ambassador, Laurence Steinhardt, convinced him that it was wrong to write off Czechoslovakia—and with it any last chance to avoid the Cold War. Returning home, Warburg pleaded with State Department officials to grant Prague credits for cotton purchases. But his private memos to the new Under Secretary of State, Robert Lovett, were politely disregarded. Either the Department had simply abandoned Czechoslovakia, or it was afraid of the effect such a credit would have on congressional attitudes toward the Marshall Plan, or both. "The gist of my reportage was that, if an Iron Curtain had been drawn around Czechoslovakia, it had been drawn by us—not by the Soviet Union."

Even as the meetings in Paris continued, Acheson returned to Truman Doctrine rhetoric in a commencement speech at Wesleyan University. The *New York Times* characterized it as a vehement denunciation of Russian foreign policy, one filled with assertions that the Soviets had unilaterally abrogated the Yalta agreements and were primarily responsible for turmoil in the Middle and Far East. Acheson also referred to the Truman Doctrine as a natural outgrowth of the Monroe Doctrine—an increasingly common practice—and combined all this with a none-too-subtle suggestion of a more active policy in Eastern Europe:

We can do, and are doing, many things. We can expose for all to see the shams and frauds behind which peoples are deprived of their liberty by little groups supported by foreign power. The methods have not changed basically since the days of Maximilian in Mexico, merely improved in organization and brutality and propaganda techniques. But they dislike exposure, and it remains to be seen whether they can survive much longer than Maximilian did the withdrawal of the foreign bayonets.

In 1947, then, Acheson preferred a bipolar world. The dynamic of the Truman Doctrine helped him to cite historical precedents for the creation of a useful past. A decade later he expanded this usable past into one that explained everything in a series of lectures titled "Power and Diplomacy."

On the one side there was the United States, reluctant leader of the free world, "primarily interested in . . . [its] own absorbing and immensely profitable affairs, and only secondarily interested in the doings and business of distant peoples." Opposed to the free world was the Soviet Union, "a revolutionary society, repudiating the most fundamental postulates of the established order, and [caught] . . . in the grip of an ideology which imbues it with unquestioning confidence in its superiority and its destined progression to triumph and dominion."

Almost everything that followed in Acheson's lectures flowed directly from these assumptions. With those of the historical main stream of the 1950's, they formed the consensus on America's entrance into world politics: the country had been forced into the arena by external explosions in Havana Harbor in 1898 (possibly in combination with an internal psychological spasm or two); but always it pulled against the forces of history, seeking some simpler life. Acheson and the "realist" diplomatic historians could agree on that, even if some of them differed with him on how to meet the Soviet challenge. Insistence upon seeing the Soviet Union as the instigator of turmoil and revolution everywhere was the main pretense of the whole ritual.

five

"red fascism" and the development of the cold war

LES K. ADLER AND THOMAS G. PATERSON

*In democratic nations, public opinion strongly influences
foreign policy. Tracing the development of American
attitudes toward the totalitarian governments of
Nazi Germany and the Soviet Union, Les K. Adler and
Thomas G. Paterson argue that the public accepted
oversimplified similarities between the two regimes and
anticipated that the Soviet Union would operate
internationally after World War II in the same way that
Germany had in the 1930s. Paterson, an associate professor
of history at the University of Connecticut, has written
extensively on the Cold War from the New Left viewpoint.
He edited* The Origins of the Cold War *(1970) and*
Cold War Critics: Alternatives to American
Foreign Policy in the Truman Years *(1971), and has
been a contributor to Bernstein (ed.),* Politics and Policies
of the Truman Administration *(1970), the* Journal of
American History, *and* The Historian; *his book* Soviet-
American Confrontation *is being published in 1973.
Both Paterson and Adler received their doctorates from
the University of California, Berkeley. Adler now teaches
at Sonoma State College and is completing a book on
the images of communism in America. Their article in the*
American Historical Review *triggered much controversy;
for criticisms of the article, and the authors replies, see the*
American Historical Review 75 *(December 1970):*

Source: Les K. Adler and Thomas G. Paterson, "Red Fascism:
The Merger of Nazi Germany and Soviet Russia in the
American Image of Totalitarianism," *American Historical Review*
75 (April 1970): 1046–64. Reprinted by permission of
the authors.

2155–64 and American Historical Review 76 *(April 1971): 575–80. Was
the American linking of the Nazi and Soviet regimes as illusory as Adler
and Paterson suggest? Do the authors minimize important similarities?*

In the early months of the cold war, Herbert L. Matthews of the New York
Times posed some disturbing questions: "Should we now place Stalinist Russia
in the same category as Hitlerite Germany? Should we say that she is Fascist?"
He answered affirmatively, as did many Americans in the post–World War II
era. President Harry S. Truman himself remarked in 1947 that "There isn't
any difference in totalitarian states. I don't care what you call them, Nazi,
Communist or Fascist. . . ." Americans both before and after the Second World
War casually and deliberately articulated distorted similarities between Nazi
and Communist ideologies, German and Soviet foreign policies, authoritarian
controls, and trade practices, and Hitler and Stalin. This popular analogy was a
potent and pervasive notion that significantly shaped American perception of
world events in the cold war. Once Russia was designated the "enemy" by
American leaders, Americans transferred their hatred for Hitler's Germany to
Stalin's Russia with considerable ease and persuasion. As Matthews put it, "It
is really a matter of labels." Those Americans who labeled Russia "Nazi
Germany" and coined the phrase "Red Fascism" were seeking relief from their
frustrated hopes for a peaceful postwar world and from their shock in finding
continued international tension after the close of a long and destructive war.
They were well acquainted with Germany; they were less familiar with
unpredictable Russia. The analogy between the two European nations provided
frightened Americans with the assurance that they knew what to expect from
Russia, because the analogy taught them and convinced them that the 1940's
and 1950's were simply a replay of the 1930's. As Marshall D. Shulman has
written, the comparison was "often misleading. . . ."

The word "totalitarianism," according to Herbert J. Spiro, "first gained
popular currency through anti-Nazi propaganda during World War II" and
"later became an anti-Communist slogan in the cold war." Americans were
almost entirely unprepared by their own national experience for giving the word
a careful definition. The term itself was an import from Europe that was
first applied to Mussolini's Italy and then to Hitler's Germany. Though coined
in the 1920's, the word did not come into general or academic use until
the late 1930's, "because the political phenomena meant to be described by it
had not attracted political attention until then." Indeed, according to
John P. Diggins, many Americans, until the Italian attack on Ethiopia and
the rise of Hitler "gave Fascism a demonic image," saw Fascist Italy as an
attractive political and social experiment. Communist leaders avoided the label
"totalitarian," partly because of their own fear and abhorrence of fascism
and partly because of their belief that "socialist democracy" better described
their own system. But in the late 1930's some anti-Communist observers began
to popularize the "totalitarianism" of Russia "as a means to emphasize certain
similarities between fascist and Communist one-party governments."

As Spiro has suggested, the propagandistic use of the term "has tended to
obscure whatever utility it may have had for systematic analysis and

comparison of political entities." Even though recognizing this problem, George F. Kennan has still argued persuasively that for totalitarianism "there are at least no *better* examples than Germany and Russia." Yet it is nevertheless true that, because the outward appearances of the two systems seemed to be more similar to each other than either seemed to be to any previous political system in the world, the real differences between fascist and Communist systems have been obscured. It was, in essence, easier for Americans to recognize their similarities than their differences, and though the intensity and scope of the analogy have varied greatly since the 1930's, the characteristic of similarity has remained constant in the American perception of totalitarian systems. Ignoring the widely diverse origins, ideologies, goals, and practices of totalitarian regimes, Americans have tended to focus only on the seemingly similar methods employed by such regimes and to assume that these methods are the basic immutable characteristics of totalitarianism anywhere.

Among the earliest to identify similarities between fascist and Communist states were a number of prominent American intellectuals who did not reflect the strong currents of pro-Soviet and profascist American thought during the late 1920's and early 1930's. In 1930 Charles Beard criticized the elitism he perceived in both fascist and Communist dictatorships; Archibald MacLeish condemned both systems in 1932 for stifling intellectual freedom; and Horace Kallen, aware of the Nazi form of fascism, castigated both systems in 1934 "for their tyrannical apotheosis of Unity." Later, after the purge trials in Russia and the persecution of the Jews in Germany, Elmer Davis, John Dewey, Walter Lippmann, George Counts, and Arthur Garfield Hays spoke out against what they considered the undemocratic, totalitarian similarities in Germany and Russia. Other Americans before the war emphasized fascist-Communist similarities. Herbert Hoover pointed out that both "are the aftermath of the gradual infection of democracy. . . ." A common theme in the *New York Times* in 1937, for example, was the unrepresentative nature of the German and Soviet governments, and Senator William Borah in the same year depicted Nazism and Communism as dogs barking at constitutional governments. Though the lack of a representative government in Russia had been a frequent point of American anti-Soviet writers since the Brest-Litovsk Treaty of 1918, Soviet secretiveness, censorship, unconcern for public opinion, purges, ideological purification, and frenzied denunciation of enemies in the 1930's seemed to echo characteristics of the Nazi regime.
Eugene Lyons, disillusioned after his failure to find a Soviet "utopia" during his visit to Russia, took his readers on a tour of European tyrannies—"totalitarian insanities"—which he equated with Russia. Everywhere he saw "the autocrats using almost the identical slogans, wielding the selfsame 'sword of history' for class or race or nation." He lamented the "moral collapse of Europe," the decline of humanistic values asserting the dignity of life and a respect for truth, and asked, "What is to distinguish socialism according to Stalin from socialism according to Mussolini?"

Like Lyons, many Americans blurred the ideological differences between Communism and fascism and tended to believe that totalitarian methods overrode the role of ideology in shaping political forms. Hans Kohn wrote forcefully against this distortion of ideology, but scholarly opinion, like public opinion increasingly moved in the opposite direction. More than a decade later Hannah Arendt argued the majority opinion persuasively in her widely praised study, *The Origins of Totalitarianism.* Miss Arendt saw a "complete indifference to mass interest" as the guiding characteristic of the "anti-utilitarian" nature of the German and Russian totalitarian regimes; yet she avoided the important distinction between one system proclaiming a humanistic ideology and failing to live up to its ideal and the other living up to its antihumanistic and destructive ideology only too well.

With the profoundly disturbing news in late August 1939 that the German *Reich* and the Soviet Union had signed a mutual nonaggression pact, and with the subsequent German and Russian invasion and division of Poland, the most significant prewar identification of the two regimes was established. Noting, like Lyons, that socialism in Germany and Russia was the same, *Collier's* magazine condemned the partition of Poland and thanked the two dictators for "dropping the pretense of hating each other's gizzards" and for removing "all doubt, except in the minds of incurable dreamers, that there is any real difference between Communism and Fascism." Some liberals, like Vincent Sheehan and Louis Fischer, who had held out hope that Russia would avoid totalitarianism, now concluded that Hitler and Stalin were full-fledged partners and, according to Sheehan, that Stalin had embraced fascism. The Reverend John Haynes Holmes, a long-time advocate of American recognition of and friendship toward the Soviet Union, reversed his stand and argued that "totalitarianism is the same everywhere . . . the leopard has the same spots in every jungle!" The liberal Presbyterian columnist, the Reverend Abraham J. Muste, surmised that the two states were anticapitalistic, anti-Christian, and antidemocratic and foresaw a "vast historical movement" toward their merger. The religious press strongly denounced the Nazi-Soviet Pact, and one Protestant minister linked their symbols in a 1939 article entitled "The Hooked Cross and the Hammer and Sickle." American Jews feared that Stalin would initiate Hitler-like policies in Poland and recalled that Russian anti-Semitism had deeper roots than that of the Germans. One Jewish journal, *The Reconstructionist,* referred to the antireligious efforts of both Russia's Militant Atheist League and Germany's Gestapo as twin attempts at "spiritual liquidation." A large segment of Catholic opinion probably agreed with *The Sign*'s characterization of Stalin, even before the pact was announced, as "far out-Hitlering Hitler in cruelty and blood-thirstiness." Father John LaFarge, writing after the pact, called the two regimes "the two greatest anti-Christian forces of the world" and recalled his earlier prediction that "Brown and Red Bolshevism" would join hands. Russia's unprovoked attack on Finland in 1939 aroused American indignation; it was, in fact, clear that both Germany and Russia were aggressors in Europe. War relief crusades for the Finns gained an ecstatic national response. Robert Sherwood responded with his well-received drama, *There Shall Be No Night,* condemning the German and Soviet aggressive conspiracy against world democracy. Frederick Hazlitt Brennan invented the phrase "Commu-Nazi" in a five-part story in early 1940 called "Let Me Call You Comrade."

Thus, on the eve of World War II, many Americans linked fascist and Communist ideologies as denials of human freedom and tolerance, saw Germany and Russia as international aggressors, and pictured Hitler and Stalin as evil comrades. Shortly after the sudden German invasion of Russia in June 1941, the *Wall Street Journal* indicated its ambivalent position on the outcome of the new war: "The American people know that the principal difference between Mr. Hitler and Mr. Stalin is the size of their respective mustaches." Former Ambassador to Russia William C. Bullitt saw the contest as one between "Satan and Lucifer." Some American isolationists denounced the power politics of both Germany and Russia and adopted a plague-on-both-your-houses attitude. Yet after the invasion President Roosevelt, against ardent opposition, promised and extended to Russia lend-lease aid. The opinion of most interventionists was that, though Russia was evil, it at least was not an immediate threat to the United States; Germany, on the other hand, was both evil and threatening. After the entry of the United States into World War II Americans focused on the differences between Hitler's Germany and Stalin's Russia in order to help cement the wartime alliance among Russia, the United States, and Great Britain. It was popular to stress that indeed Russia and the United States were similar; both were anti-imperialist, and both had a revolutionary past. *Collier's* in 1943 could conclude that Russia was "evolving from a sort of Fascism . . . toward something resembling our own and Great Britain's democracy." But the stress on differences was a temporary façade, a reaction to Soviet war efforts rather than a reappraisal, and the Nazi-Communist analogy appeared publicly again as Soviet-American tensions increased near the close of the war.

Even before the war ended, W. Averell Harriman suggested to Secretary of the Navy James Forrestal that the thrust of Communism was not dead and that indeed the United States might have to confront an ideological war perhaps as "vigorous and dangerous as Fascism or Nazism." Acting Secretary of State Joseph C. Grew sent President Truman a briefing paper in June 1945 stating that "Communists have the same attitude as Goebbels did—that the civil liberties of the democracies are convenient instruments for Communists to facilitate their tearing down the structure of the state and thereafter abolishing all civil rights." To those who ridiculed his subsequent call for a study of Soviet philosophy, Forrestal replied that "we always should remember that we also laughed at Hitler." A New Hampshire lawyer, later to be that state's Attorney General and congressman, asked in 1946, "Do you remember that Hitler's plans were fully outlined in his book *Mein Kampf* and that no one paid serious attention?" The Russians had never retracted their plans for world revolution, and he urged Americans to beware. One prominent businessman condemned both Germany and Russia and argued that "any system that doesn't put a penalty on inactivity and a reward on activity is bound to fail." The Economic Cooperation Administration concluded that both Hitler and the Cominform were international liars; the president of International Harvester linked Russia and Germany as the twentieth-century "forces of slavery"; and "Red-fascism" was introduced into American political parlance.

In totalitarian states, Americans were aware, absolute control over the means of communication gave the regime the ability to grant people access only to the information it wished them to have. Germany had controlled information, and Secretary Grew told a nationwide radio audience in June 1945 that "never again must a tyranny be permitted to mislead and befuddle a people and to betray men and women into mob violence, aggression and national suicide." Many Americans in the postwar period believed that Russia's control of communications, information, and propaganda were replicas of the German model, and many assumed that aggressive war would be the inevitable result of an absence of free expression. Assistant Secretary of State William Benton, offering a rationale for American propaganda efforts through the Voice of America in 1947, maintained that "we have learned that there is an essential connection between denial of freedom of expression on the one hand, and dictatorship and war on the other." And it was evident to many American leaders that Russian propaganda was comparable to that of Goebbels.

Mental and physical regimentation as a characteristic of totalitarianism was assumed by General John R. Deane, the head of the American military mission in wartime Russia. In his much-publicized *Strange Alliance* Deane drew heavily on the Nazi-Soviet analogy. He noted that the marching of Russian soldiers "closely resembled the goose-step, with arms rigid and legs kicked stiffly to the front," and this "pointed plainly to a discipline oriented toward German methods, which tends to destroy individual initiative in the battle pay off." Deane also related this regimentation to the control of ideas. "Unfortunately the Russian people are not allowed to see that the pattern being cut by their leaders is much the same as that which was followed in Germany." President Lewis H. Brown of the Johns-Manville Corporation agreed that "the Russian people, like the German people, do not want to rule the world, but they are helpless slaves of the ruling clique that dominates the people through fear and terror, through concentration camps and secret police and through the whole mechanism of totalitarianism."

Control through fear and terror was, indeed, a significant component of the totalitarian image perceived by Americans. Americans knew of Russian exile and labor camps in Siberia even before the Bolshevik revolution in 1917, and in the 1920's and 1930's it was known that such camps were filled with political prisoners, criminals, and those opposed to the Soviet collectivization schemes. The German experience, however, seems to have stamped the image of the concentration camp, with all its overtones of mass extermination and unbridled terror, on the Russian camps. Congresswoman Clare Boothe Luce in 1946 castigated the Soviet system as one "which keeps eighteen million people out of 180 million in concentration and forced labor camps." In the United Nations, the American representative, Willard L. Thorp, compared the "shocking exploitation of human beings by the Nazis" with alleged forced labor conditions in Russia. In 1947 Senator J. Howard McGrath, later Truman's Attorney General, applied the analogy of concentration camps to Eastern Europe and found that in Yugoslavia alone "over 400,000 believers in God and freedom have been killed, and 100,000 are in prisons and concentration camps." Citing as his source of information the vehemently anti-Communist publication *Plain Talk* and the writings of strongly anti-Soviet writers such as William C.

Bullitt and Leon Dennen, McGrath also claimed that the clergy in Estonia, Latvia, Lithuania, and Yugoslavia were being exterminated. The image of Nazi death camps was thus conjured up. Arthur Bliss Lane, American ambassador to Poland from 1945 to 1947, added that the Russian security police copied Gestapo tactics. Speaking of persons brutally beaten and tortured by police, Lane told a radio audience that "the same terror of a knock at the door in the dead of night exists today as it did during the Nazi occupation." Such suppression of human liberties and terror "are, in my opinion, as horrible to the American people whether they are permitted under the emblem of the Swastika or under the emblem of the Hammer and Sickle." The St. Louis Trust Company swept over history in its indictment: "Systematic race persecution in Germany and class persecution in Russia serve the same purposes as the Roman circuses, gladiatorial contests and persecution of the early Christians." President Truman summarized the question simply in 1950 when he concluded that "there isn't any difference between the totalitarian Russian government and the Hitler government. . . . They are all alike. They are police governments—police state governments."

Americans pointed out too that both fascist and Communist regimes attempted to extend their ideological appeal and brute tactics to other nations through subversive agents. Disclosures of and allegations against suspected spies in Canada and the United States inflated fears of foreign agents. Francis P. Matthews, a director of the United States Chamber of Commerce and the originator of a series of influential anti-Communist publications by that organization, indicated to the chamber's board of directors that in his pamphlets "what we say about Communists, applies with equal force to Fascist, Nazi or any other agents of foreign powers who follow similar tactics." After this comparison, he added, "We restrict the discussion to Communists for the reason that the greatest current danger, now that the Fascist and Nazi axis was defeated in World War II, comes from the Communists." Matthews feared Communist infiltration into American labor unions, mass media, and the federal government. Thus all Communists, like all fascists, who owed a "superior loyalty to a foreign power" should be excluded from government employment and from other sensitive positions. Attorney General Tom C. Clark concurred in a speech in 1946 to the Chicago Bar Association, pointing out that "we know that there is a national and international conspiracy to divide our people, to discredit our institutions, and to bring about disrespect for our government." After all, "we know full well what communism and fascism practice—sometimes one taking the cloak of the other."

As Americans perceived an increasing postwar threat from Russia and as the threat of Germany subsided and, indeed, the United States began to court that country as an ally, many saw Communism as an even greater menace than fascism had been. Americans credited Soviet Communists with better "fifth-column" activities. In June 1945 the State Department informed the President that "a communist party was in fact a fifth column as much as any Bund group, except that the latter were crude and ineffective in comparison with Communists." Blinded by the analogy, American leaders could only perceive the civil war in Greece as a Hitler-like fifth-column intrusion by the Russians and not, as it was in reality, a struggle of Greeks against a British-supported monarchy with little interference by the Soviet Union. When appearing before Congress to ask for funds for the economic development of Latin America, Spruille Braden testified that Communists in that region were a greater peril than "Nazi columnists," because the Communists infiltrated all political movements—even the conservative ones—but the Germans had been less able to integrate themselves into Latin American national life. Congressman Charles A. Eaton wrote in 1947 that the Russian "fifth column in the United States is greater than Hitler's fifth column ever was." And the former head of the Office of Strategic Services, General William J. Donovan, added in 1948 that "the Nazis exploited 'the disqualified and the traitors' on a large scale; the Soviets have enlarged and perfected that technique."

Perhaps the most significant, and the most misleading, part of the Nazi-Communist analogy was that drawn between the prewar and wartime military actions of Germany and those of Russia in the postwar period. As Soviet armies marched into Eastern Europe on the heels of the defeated *Wehrmacht,* many Americans perceived it as immediate aggression rather than as wartime liberation. A clear example of this process was the early transposition of the American vocabulary applied to the Nazi domination of Europe. It was assumed, without understanding the Soviet security concerns or its national interest, that Russia was simply replacing Germany as the disrupter of peace in Europe. The term "satellite," first applied to German domination of Rumania and Hungary, was easily transferred to Russian hegemony in postwar Eastern Europe. Winston Churchill, who helped popularize the notion in America, lumped Germany and Russia together as similar aggressors, and Max Eastman and the Russian *émigré* Ely Culbertson both condemned Russia for employing the German practice of disregarding treaties and adopting satellite states. H. V. Kaltenborn, shortly after Churchill's famous iron curtain speech in 1946, bluntly labeled the Soviet Union "a ruthless, totalitarian power which is seeking domination in both Europe and Asia," and he warned his radio listeners to "Remember Munich!" George V. Allen of the State Department stated in 1949 that both Russia and Germany were responsible for the collapse of the League of Nations. "Aggression, if it comes, will destroy the United Nations as surely as it destroyed the League. And in totalitarianism, of either the right or the left, lie the seeds of aggressive action."

It was thus the view of many leading Americans that Russia, like Germany before, was going to sweep over Europe in a massive military attack. Lewis H. Brown argued that Russia "is the dread of every family in Western Europe every night when they go to bed." Such sentiment encouraged the formation of the North Atlantic Treaty Organization and other regional alliances. J. Howard McGrath anticipated the arguments in 1947 when he told the Senate: "Today it is Trieste, Korea, and Manchuria, tomorrow it is the British Empire. The next day it is South America. And then—who is so blind as to fail to see the next step?" In 1948 Secretary of State George C. Marshall recalled his prewar experience of watching "the Nazi government take control of one country after another until finally Poland was invaded in a direct military operation." His words clearly suggested the parallel with postwar Russia.

George F. Kennan, the State Department expert on the Soviet Union in
Moscow and Washington considered by most observers as the architect of the
containment policy, attempted in 1956 to dispel a myth that he himself had
helped create years earlier. "The image of a Stalinist Russia," he argued,
"poised and yearning to attack the West, and deterred only by our possession of
atomic weapons, was largely a creation of the Western imagination." Kennan
has claimed that the containment doctrine he advocated in private and in
his influential "X" article in the July 1947 issue of *Foreign Affairs* did not
suggest forceful containment, the creation of a ring of military bases and
alliances around Russia, or an identification of German aggression with Russian
presence in Eastern Europe. Yet popularizers of the Nazi-Soviet analogy in
official Washington and elsewhere used Kennan, in part because of his own
imprecision in 1947, to argue their case that Russian "aggression" had to be
halted or America would face another world war. Protesting what he considered
to be the misuse of his ideas, Kennan could only conclude that "Washington's
reactions" had been "deeply subjective."

"Munich" and "appeasement" returned as terms of humiliation and shame
to haunt postwar negotiations with the Soviet Union. Responding to Roosevelt's
agreement at Yalta to allow the Soviet Union three votes in the United Nations
General Assembly, Senator Arthur Vandenberg indicated that among the
members of the American delegation to the San Francisco United Nations
meeting "there is a general disposition to *stop this Stalin appeasement. It has*
to stop *sometime.* Every surrender makes it more difficult." In defending the
Truman Doctrine in 1947, Vandenberg remarked that "I think the adventure
is worth trying as an alternative to another 'Munich' and perhaps to another
war. . . ." To the suggestion made at a cabinet meeting in September 1945 that
the United States eliminate its monopoly of atomic bombs and nuclear
information in the interests of peace, Secretary Forrestal replied that "it seems
doubtful that we should endeavor to buy their understanding and sympathy.
We tried that once with Hitler. There are no returns on appeasement."
Barron's chastised Henry Wallace in 1946 for his advocacy of disarmament in
atomic weapons through an agreement with Russia and wrote that he had
an "appeaser's dream." In 1950 General Douglas MacArthur considered the
policy of containing rather than unleashing Chiang Kai-shek to be
"appeasement," and he chastised those in the administration who would not
escalate the Korean War, for they were adhering to "the concept of appeasement,
the concept that when you use force, you can limit the force." Adlai Stevenson,
in the 1952 presidential campaign, argued that a withdrawal of American
troops to allow "Asians to fight Asians . . . would risk a Munich in the
Far East, with the possibility of a third world war not far behind." Since
the cry of appeasement was pervasive in the American mind, diplomats may
have been less willing to bargain and more willing to adopt uncompromising
positions vis-à-vis the Soviet Union. Indeed, for some, diplomacy and
appeasement were probably nearly identical in meaning, and diplomacy with
totalitarian states meant concession to principle. This national stance was
suggested by President Truman in his Navy Day speech of October 1945 when
he stated that "we shall firmly adhere to what we believe to be right; and

we shall not give our approval to any compromise with evil." Such an attitude had a paralyzing effect on international give and take and certainly impeded the accommodation of international differences.

The publication by the State Department on January 21, 1948, of captured German documents concerning the Nazi-Soviet Pact of 1939 fed the notion that Russia was aggressive, deceitful, and opportunistic, and that consequently the United States must deal sternly from a position of power with the Communist nation. Walter Lippmann thought that publication "the work of propagandists and not of scholars," but most commentators, as unaware in 1948 as they had been in 1938 of the intricacies of national interest and diplomacy, read the documents as the validation of the charge that the Nazis and the Russians had been essentially one and the same in their aims of world conquest. Dorothy Thompson was baffled that the American government had gone ahead with the United Nations Charter and the Nuremberg Trials "with the Russians sitting as prosecutors and judges against the very persons they had egged on to war and with whom they had plotted to divide the spoils." Ignoring the history of Russia's rebuffed efforts to form an anti-German coalition with the West in the 1930's—an ignorance reinforced by the selected published documents—the New York *Times* editorialized on the basis of the German documents alone that "the initiative toward the conspiracy did not come from the Nazis, but from Moscow, behind the backs of France and Britain," and Bertram D. Hulen of the New York *Times* thought the documents proved that Soviet officials "would rather work with the Germans than with the West." Kaltenborn believed the publication of the documents in early 1948 was a maneuver by the Truman administration to scare Congress into passing Marshall Plan legislation, but Secretary Marshall himself said the publication was routine and had in fact been postponed pending the results of the Foreign Ministers' Conference of December 1947 in order not to offend the Russians. With the failure of the meeting, the documents were released. More important than the question of the timing of publication is that of the significance of these diplomatic sources to the development of American thought on the cold war. The documents reinforced and reflected the American image of the Nazi-Soviet connection and strengthened the argument of those who believed that Russia had never shared Allied war goals, but rather embraced the German aims of world domination.

An additional component of the Nazi-Soviet comparison was presented by commentators on international trade. Russia in the postwar world conducted foreign trade through the agency of the government, as had Germany before. Both, it was suggested, used trade for political purposes, and both imposed harsh commercial treaties on Eastern European countries. Germany and Russia thus forced weaker nations to buy goods at exorbitant prices and to sell products to them at reduced rates. Trade, then, was another weapon in the aggressive arsenal of totalitarian states. Recalling American trade with Germany and Japan before the war, Kennan stated in 1945 that there was little to gain, and much to lose, from postwar American-Russian trade. By trading with postwar Russia, he reasoned, Americans might be "furthering the military industrialization of the Soviet Union" and "be creating military strength which

might some day be used to our disadvantage. . . ." His suggestion was clear
that prewar American trade with the Axis Powers had served to build up
the enemy against the United States and that postwar Russian-American trade
might replay such events. This type of thinking again forced rigidity upon
postwar American foreign policy because it assumed that the course of
relations was already set and that the prewar decade provided an accurate map
for the postwar era.

Americans after the Second World War also blended their images of the
German *Führer* and the Soviet Premier. Stalin was a new Hitler, demagogic,
dictatorial, demanding personal loyalty, conniving to rule other peoples. The
tough but friendly "Uncle Joe" of wartime propaganda became the paranoid
tyrant of the cold war, aping Hitler. The president of the University of
Notre Dame articulated the widely held assumption that Stalin was continuing
Hitler's viciousness. *Iron Age* concluded that "Stalin has succeeded to the
mantle of Hitler as a menace to world peace." George Meany of the American
Federation of Labor called Stalin "the Russian Hitler," and General Donovan
believed that Stalin was in fact more ruthless and thorough than the *Führer*.

In 1949 Professor Leo Szilard of the University of Chicago wrote in the
Bulletin of Atomic Scientists: "Soviet Russia is a dictatorship no less ruthless
perhaps than was Hitler's dictatorship in Germany. Does it follow that Russia
will act as Hitler's Germany acted?" Szilard did not think so, and his question
emphasizes at once the major assumption and the major weakness of the
Nazi-Communist analogy: that conflict with totalitarianism was inevitable after
World War II; that there was no room for accommodation with the Soviet
Union because the Communist nation was inexorably driven by its ideology and
its totalitarianism. It followed from such reasoning that the United States
could have done nothing to alleviate postwar tension. Such a notion, however,
ignores the important years 1945–1946 when the possibilities for accommodation
were far greater than later in the decade. The analogy itself obstructed
accommodation: it did not allow for a sophisticated understanding of power
relationships in Europe; it substituted emotion for intellect; and it particularly
affected the American perception of reality. There were, without question,
similarities between Nazi Germany and Communist Russia. But to assume that
the similarity was total, as did many leading Americans, was to miss the
particular differences which perhaps left an opening for an early peaceful
coexistence. What is more important for this discussion, however, is not that
they were different, but that many Americans took the unhistorical and illogical
view that Russia in the 1940's would behave as Germany had in the previous
decade.

Of prominent American political figures in the early postwar era, a few men
like Henry Wallace consistently refuted the analogy and asked simply how
America could deal with the reality of Russian hegemony in Eastern Europe,
a hegemony Wallace defined as defensive rather than aggressive or offensive.
Wallace wrote to Truman in July 1946 that Russia had legitimate security needs
in Europe. "We should be prepared," he asserted, "even at the expense of
risking epithets of appeasement, to agree to reasonable Russian guarantees of
security." The United States, in short, could not expect Russia to relinquish its

national interest, any more than anyone would expect the British to ignore what they considered to be British national interest in Greece, or the United States to abandon Latin America. Professors Fred Neal and Frederick Schuman, among others, have suggested that, in fact, much Soviet foreign policy after the Second World War was defensive and cautious and that there is no imperative in the Communist ideology for military aggression. Neal points out that Americans have misread the Communist belief that capitalism will collapse as meaning Communist military conquest of the world. Americans drew little distinction between the German drive for European domination and the Soviet interest in revolution—between military attack and internal revolution. The Marxian philosophy looked for social and economic improvement among disadvantaged people, whereas, as Hans Buchheim has suggested, fascism was designed not to improve mankind, but rather to destroy that part it disliked. Wolfgang Sauer recently wrote that "Neither V. I. Lenin nor Joseph Stalin wished to turn the clock back; they not merely wished to move ahead, but they wished to jump ahead. The Bolshevik revolution had many elements of a development revolution not unlike those now under way in the underdeveloped countries." The American failure to note distinctions between military fascism and revolutionary Marxism has contributed to a simplistic view of revolutionary and anticolonial movements in the post–World War II era and has led to the establishment of world-wide alliances and permanent military containment policies in Europe and Asia. As Professor Robert F. Smith has written, "This distorted use of historical analogy vastly oversimplifies not only the policies of Russia and China, but also the nationalistic reform movements around the world."

The Hitler-Stalin comparison has also been superficial and misleading. Sauer has written that "the social and political order of Bolshevism is relatively independent from the leadership. . . . Fascist regimes, by contrast, are almost identical with their leaders; no fascist regime has so far survived its leader." Kennan himself attempted to convince his readers in 1956 that Stalin's intentions, though menacing in Western eyes, were "not to be confused with the reckless plans and military timetable of a Hitler." Brutal and idiosyncratic as Stalin was, there is little evidence, as Kennan has indicated, to suggest that he was a madman bent on world conquest and subjugation. In his recent massive and penetrating study of Soviet foreign policy, Adam B. Ulam concludes that "Soviet leaders sensibly enough concentrated on the area deemed of direct importance to the Soviet Union: eastern and southeastern Europe. They avoided any appearance of a many-sided attack on the Old World's positions that would increase American suspicions and countermeasures." There was no Soviet "blueprint" for the postwar period.

In short, the analogy taught that the enigma of Soviet Russia could be fathomed only by the application of the historical lesson learned in the 1930's. Indeed, as distinguished scholars have written in the postwar period, totalitarian systems have exhibited undeniable similarities. Yet it did not follow that Russia and Stalin in the cold war would always act in a manner similar to Germany and Hitler or that Russia was set inexorably on the path of military aggression. Many Americans thought the conclusion did follow; they ultimately concluded that it was useless to negotiate or to compromise with the Russians and that it was quite necessary to adopt an inflexible, "get-tough" policy toward them.

The American image of "Red Fascism" embraced emotion and simplism, and the compelling fictional creations and antiutopias of writers such as George Orwell, Aldous Huxley, and Arthur Koestler helped foster the crude and superficial analogy. Orwell's *1984,* appearing at the time when American fears of totalitarianism had become obsessive, did much to shape American thought and opinion. For serious scholars and casual readers alike, the image of totalitarianism presented in *1984* has been a model, as unreal and probably as significant as that created by American leaders and the mass media from the war's end to the book's publication in America in 1949. So closely had the Nazi-Soviet image been woven into American thought that it proved difficult for many Americans to read the book without applying totalitarian stereotypes from the Nazi-Soviet analogy. A *Life* editorial, reprinted along with a condensed version of the book in *Reader's Digest,* for example, found the book "so good, indeed, so full of excitement and horror, that there is some danger that its message will be ignored." Clarifying the novel's message, *Life*'s editors unhesitatingly identified the central and alarming figure of "Big Brother" as a "mating" of Hitler and Stalin and made it clear that Russia and Germany were to be substituted for the author's obvious use of London as the novel's setting, an interpretation perhaps more indicative of American perception than of Orwell's own intentions.

It was in Kennan's introspective mind, however, that the impact of the total analogy and total image was best understood and articulated. Well aware of the component parts of the analogy, many of which he believed with the majority of Americans, Kennan also recognized the additional dream-like quality that the Red-fascist image had taken on in the American mind:

When I try to picture totalitarianism to myself as a general phenomenon, what comes into my mind most prominently is neither the Soviet picture nor the Nazi picture as I have known them in the flesh, but rather the fictional and symbolic images created by such people as Orwell or Kafka or Koestler or the early Soviet satirists. The purest expression of the phenomenon, in other words, seems to me to have been rendered not in its physical reality but in its power as a dream, or a nightmare. Not that it lacks the physical reality, or that this reality is lacking in power; but it is precisely in the way it appears to people, in the impact it has on the subconscious, in the state of mind it creates in its victims, that totalitarianism reveals most deeply its meaning and nature. Here, then, we seem to have a phenomenon of which it can be said that it is both a reality and a bad dream, but that its deepest reality lies strangely enough in its manifestation as a dream. . . .

This nightmare of "Red Fascism" terrified a generation of Americans and left its mark on the events of the cold war and its warriors.

part two
american policy and the cold war in transition, 1953–62

six
the "thaw" of
1953-1955

LOUIS J. HALLE

Louis J. Halle, director of the Institute of International
Studies in Geneva, Switzerland, has been deeply involved
in American foreign policy, both as a participant in
its formulation and as a scholarly critic. Halle was born
in 1901 and studied at Harvard University. From
1941 to 1954 he worked in the Department of State,
prinicipally in inter-American relations, and during the
years from 1952 to 1954 served on the Policy
Planning Staff. In addition to The Cold War as History
(1967), from which the following selection is taken,
Halle's works include Civilization and Foreign
Policy *(1955),* Choice for Survival *(1958),* Dream and
Reality *(1959), and* Men and Nations *(1962). In*
The Cold War as History *Halle reveals a certain*
disenchantment with the diplomacy of the Eisenhower
administration. Like the majority of political
analysts, Halle accepts as fact that after Stalin's death in
1953 Russia began to pursue the idea of coexistence.
But the government, he believes, was so convinced
of Russia's intent, by whatever means, to establish its
political system throughout the world that it moved too
cautiously in responding to changes in Soviet policy.
Considering the development of doctrinaire American
attitudes toward Russia which the Bernstein, Gardner, and
Adler-Paterson essays underscore, does Halle expect too
much by way of fundamental change in American
policy? Given Halle's view that the Cold War could not
be ended in the mid-fifties, and the sparse accomplishments

Source: Louis J. Halle, *The Cold Was as History* (New York:
Harper & Row, 1967), pp. 312–18, 320–24, 331–35.
Copyright © 1967 by Louis J. Halle. Reprinted by permission
of Harper & Row, Publishers, Inc.

of the high-level conferences, was the American restraint and
reluctance justifiable?

In his airgram of February 22, 1946, from Moscow, George Kennan had
written: "It has yet to be demonstrated that [the Soviet system] can survive
supreme test of successive transfer of power from one individual or group to
another. Lenin's death was the first such transfer, and its effects wracked Soviet
state for 15 years after. Stalin's death or retirement will be second." In the seven
years that followed, a constant topic of speculation and discussion, inside and
outside of Government, had been: After Stalin, what? Only the inhibition
against 'wishful thinking' held in check the hope, widespread throughout the
West, that the Soviet state, unable to resolve the problem of the succession,
would fall into confusion and helplessness upon Stalin's removal from the
scene. Surely this might have happened. In the absence of effective constitutional
provisions establishing the procedures of succession—provisions that cannot
exist in connection with illegitimate personal rule—the door was open to
anarchy. Beria, overthrown in Moscow, might have found refuge in Georgia,
which he had been converting into a personal stronghold; and civil war might
have ensued. Or he might have seized power in Moscow and found that he
could maintain it only by the practice of such terrorism as would itself have
spelled chaos. Or the Army might have moved against the Party, or against the
secret police, with incalculable consequences.

Even from the standpoint of the Soviet regime's enemies it is doubtful that
anarchy over the vast realm of Russia was desirable. Anarchy tends to propagate
itself. The breakdown of authority in the Soviet Union would have been
followed, immediately, by a breakdown of authority throughout the eastern half
of Europe. There might have been violent clashes between rival leaders with their
respective followers. There would surely have been interventions across state
frontiers, probably amounting to invasions. Perhaps the Poles would have
undertaken to reconquer the territory they had lost to Russia in 1944 and 1945.
Perhaps the Chinese would have moved to occupy Siberia and Outer Mongolia.
Perhaps the Germans would have crossed the Oder-Neisse line. Perhaps the
Greeks and Yugoslavs would have clashed over Bulgarian Macedonia. Under
such circumstances of spreading anarchy the West would have been drawn
irresistibly into East Europe to provide rescue, to forestall rivals, to re-establish
order. Who knows what clashes this, in turn, might have led to? Anarchy in
Russia would have been like a fire spreading in a dry forest.

If one takes account of political possibilities one is bound to conclude, I think,
that what actually happened in Russia, upon the removal of Stalin, was about the
best that could have been expected. Control was kept by relatively responsible
men who, as it later transpired, were animated by a genuine revulsion against
what Stalin had represented.

As the months lengthened into years, moreover, it became apparent that in the
era of Stalin's rule Russia had undergone an evolution by which such rule itself
had been rendered increasingly obsolete. The Russian society had been
outgrowing its traditional barbarism. With industrialization—which had been
advancing rapidly under the czars and had continued under their successors—a

relatively sophisticated class of industrial managers and technicians had been rising to predominance. These men, whose role was indispensable, could not function under the conditions that, for a thousand years, had kept the Russian people in a state of servitude approaching that of domestic animals. They were not, like their forebears, illiterate peasants. Their role and their willingness to perform it required widespread freedom of debate and decision. And their training made them as apt to question political authority as to accept it. Russian scientists and scholars, upon whom the society depended more and more, had the same requirements and predilections in even greater degree. All this meant that the days when Russia could be ruled by an Ivan the Terrible or a Stalin were at their end.

The collective leaders appear to have appreciated this. They were, it seems, determined that a Caligula should not succeed to a Caligula. The principle of moderation had enough credit among them, and they had enough respect for orderly procedures, so that they were unwilling to settle their rivalries by assassination or mete out death to the losers as Stalin had done. The death of Beria, since it was the product of a secret trial on essentially political charges, must be accounted an exception; but what is notable is the fact that it was so. When Khrushchev, in successive maneuvers, defeated Malenkov, Molotov, Kaganovich, Bulganin, and Zhukov, he simply sent them into a comfortable retirement. And when he himself was overthrown in 1964 the like consideration was shown to him. This represented a hopeful improvement on the Byzantine tradition that Stalin had embodied. I doubt that many observers at the beginning of 1953 foresaw it.

The years that followed Stalin's death also showed that important aspects of his foreign policy were without honor in the minds of his successors. He had dangerously overextended the empire of which they found themselves the heirs. He had then united the West against it, provoking the restoration of West Europe under the leadership of the United States. He had alienated Yugoslavia, thereby producing the first great break in the Communist front. He had blundered in Korea, with incalculable consequences that included the rearmament of the nations banded together in the Atlantic alliance. In a world of nuclear weapons his conduct of foreign relations had raised international tensions to a point of extreme danger for the Soviet state. The new leadership, although it could not expect to disengage from the Cold War and so bring it to an end in the immediate future, this being beyond the bounds of political possibility, showed itself anxious to relax international tensions and to retrench the overextended empire where it could be retrenched without too much danger.

The fundamental change that all this represented was not only unappreciated in the United States, where the movement of opinion had been away from moderation, but was almost wilfully disregarded. As had been the case when the Japanese had been trying, a decade earlier, to find a way out of World War II, no one in Washington dared to accept the apparent new attitudes of the demonic enemy at face value. McCarthyism, beginning at the end of 1949, had only now achieved the heights of its supremacy, and anyone who suggested that Stalin's death had diminished the menace of the Communist conspiracy was likely to find himself suspect. He would, in any case, be silenced by the outspokenness of the opinion against him. Everyone agreed that no one must allow himself to be misled by the smiles of the new Communist leadership. Everyone felt impelled to make it clear how little he, in any case, was in danger of being taken in by them.

Just below the surface of consciousness in Washington there were powerful reasons for such a reaction to the outward appearances of a new moderation in Moscow. By 1953 the entire foreign policy of the United States, so painfully developed after 1946, was based on the Cold War. It made sense only in terms of the premises on which the Cold War was being fought. Specifically, the policy was based on the belief that Moscow was determined, by fraud or violence, to establish its ideology, its political system, and its domination over the entire world. The men in Washington, as a group, were the authors of that policy. They had created it, they had developed it, they had struggled to gain its acceptance by the American people. It was their baby. They were bound to react with alarm, now, to any suggestion that the premises of their policy might no longer be valid —just because there were smiles in Moscow where before there had been frowns.

More specifically, the United States was, at this time, making every effort to persuade its European allies that the Soviet menace was such as to require greatly increased contributions by them to the military forces being assembled under NATO; and that the danger was of such magnitude as to make the organization of a European Defense Community imperative. This was precisely the period when the United States was putting pressure on France to ratify the E.D.C. Treaty. All this effort would be defeated, now, if the Europeans should be so gullible as to believe that, just because the Russians were smiling, the danger had passed. The tendency, therefore, was to become still more shrill in pointing out the danger and in rallying the troops.

Finally, any great struggle like the Cold War creates vested interests beyond those that represent intellectual commitment alone. In the United States the top staffs of the three military services have to give a major portion of their time, year in year out, to preparing their requests for appropriations and to fighting their case for those requests through the various committees and subcommittees of both houses of Congress. They find themselves asking the Congressmen for the largest possible budgets on the basis of the magnitude of the foreign danger they have to meet. It is not their business to underestimate that danger. On the contrary, they are moved to present, as the basis for their requirements, the most extreme estimates of the antagonist's intentions and capabilities. If, now, Moscow's smiles should be taken seriously, the military chiefs would see their budgets reduced by the forces in Congress that favored economy and that now saw an opportunity to practice it. (There is no question here of the honesty of the military leaders: like human beings in other situations of the sort, they genuinely believe in what conforms to the interests with which they identify themselves, interests that in this case are directly identified, in turn, with the national interest.)

Finally, there is the vast industrial complex, constituting a substantial part of the nation's economy, that depends on Government contracts. Those who produce war materials have a vested interest no less marked than that of the military in the menace to the national security, and are no less sincere in their defense of it. They, too, identifying their professional interests with the national interest, were bound to view with alarm any tendency to minimize the Soviet menace in response to smiles from Moscow.

For several years after Stalin's death, then, the orthodox saying in Washington, when the matter came under discussion, was that the new regime in Russia was even more dangerous than the old because, by its smiles, it threatened to betray the West into "letting down its guard."

Inside the State Department the intelligence specialists on Soviet affairs, who regularly briefed the Secretary of State and his entourage, continued for at least a year and a half after Stalin's death to report that the succession represented no significant change in the objectives, the policies, or the basic attitudes of Moscow. Everything was essentially as it had been under Stalin. Continuity was unbroken.

Roberta Wohlstetter, referring to the conclusions that the intelligence experts draw from the factual data that they gather and collate, has observed that "without a very large and complete body of assumptions and estimates, the data collected would not speak to us at all."[1] This is fundamental. No meaning can be elicited from unordered accumulations of factual data until they have been arranged in accordance with a conceptual framework that, in the realm of politics, represents for the most part such assumptions as it occurs to no one to question. It is common experience that we interpret the behavior of one whom we regard as a friend quite differently from the interpretation we would put on identical behavior in one whom we regarded as an enemy, simply because we make different assumptions about him. Presumably the Soviet intelligence experts interpret the data that they gather according to the tenets of Marxism-Leninism.

The tacit assumption that the intelligence experts in Washington made, when they set themselves to interpret the vast arrays of data before them, was that of a conspiratorial movement for the overthrow of capitalist society, founded by Marx and Engels a century earlier, which had been pursuing its fixed purpose with unalterable determination through successive generations to the present. The movement was one of men who were dedicated and disciplined, so that when one of them fell the others would immediately close ranks and carry on. Marx, Lenin, Stalin, Mao Tse-tung, Ho Chi Minh, Khrushchev—all were the servants of the one continuing movement. If there were from time to time variations in their conduct of the movement these represented tactical maneuvers only. Khrushchev's call for an international *détente,* for "peaceful coexistence" of the "socialist and capitalist camps," was such a maneuver, designed to seduce our allies and to throw us off our guard. In the light of these basic assumptions, the figures on steel-production, the latest data on the development of the Russian aircraft industry, a reorganization of Red Army units, a statement in a Russian technical journal—all fitted together to show that the succession to Stalin had brought no real change.

This conclusion began to be increasingly difficult to maintain, however, after the middle of 1955, when the new regime in Moscow had withdrawn the Red Army from East Austria, abondoning the occupation that it had been maintaining there as in East Germany; when it had publicly apologized to Tito for the errors of its predecessor, and had publicly agreed with him that each socialist state had

---

[1] Roberta Wohlstetter, "Cuba and Pearl Harbor," *Foreign Affairs* 43 (July 1965): 706.

the right to follow its own path to socialism without interference from outside; when it had evacuated Port Arthur and had returned to Finland the naval base of Porkkala; when it had taken the initiative to recognize the German Federal Republic and establish normal relations with it; when it had moved to normalize its relations with Japan; and when it had made notable concessions to the Western powers on the issue of disarmament. It became impossible to maintain after the text of Khrushchev's denunciation of Stalin and Stalinism at the 20th Party Congress in February 1956 became known.

The more generous and liberal line that Moscow pursued in foreign affairs after Stalin's death (and which had been foreshadowed at the 19th Party Congress before his death) could be discounted as representing simply a decision to pause in its career of world conquest, and to reduce, pending the completion of its own nuclear armament, the danger to itself inherent in the excessively high tensions that had been allowed to develop under Stalin. It was proper, as a matter of prudence, that one should so discount these changes. After all, Germany was still divided, Berlin was still besieged, East Europe was still under the tyranny of Moscow. Nevertheless, the changes, whatever motives they represented, were real changes, and they were not insignificant from the practical point of view. In international relations, what one does now is more important than what one may intend to do at some time in the future. Decisions made with respect to some time in the future are not operative. It is not until the future time comes that the operative decision will be made, and it will not necessarily conform to what had been projected earlier. Without prematurely abandoning its defenses, the West could properly recognize the change and explore its possibilities. This, in fact, is what it would begin to do in the summer of 1955. . . .

In his airgram of February 22, 1946, Kennan had written: "Soviet internal system will now be subjected, by virtue of recent territorial expansions, to a series of additional strains which once proved severe tax on Tsardom." The cruder view that came to prevail in Washington was that the Russian state had been immensely strengthened by the acquisition of all the populations and natural resources of East Europe—and, after 1949, of China too. One may plausibly believe, however, that if Stalin's successors had spoken frankly they would have confirmed what Kennan had written. . . .

The difficulties and dangers of Moscow's overextension were dramatized for the new leaders by certain developments in East Europe during the months after Stalin's death. Early in June 1953 there were insurrectionary uprisings against Russian domination and the Communist regime in Czechoslovakia. In East Germany on June 24 the puppet Prime Minister, Grotewohl, made a speech in which he admitted that the flight of "hundreds of thousands" of farmers to the West had caused serious food shortages. During that same month there was a spontaneous general uprising of the people in East Berlin, demanding liberation from the Russians and an end to Communist rule. This insurrection spread to cities all over East Germany. The local police forces were unable to cope with it, so that the Russians were compelled to use their own tanks and troops to put it down if East Germany was not to break away and join the West.

The new Russian leaders were confronted by the fact that the same explosive situation existed throughout their East European empire, where they were trying to hold a lid on a volcano. One can imagine the alarm among them at the possibility of Western intervention to support uprisings of the captive peoples, and at the prospect of what would happen throughout East Europe if war with the West should break out. They might have tried to deal with this danger by multiplying their means of suppression, by intensifying the reign of terror. But a reign of terror merely increases disaffection and thereby aggravates the long-term problem. The alternative was to appease the disaffected peoples by providing improved conditions of living, and by cautiously relaxing the suppressive measures to which they were being subjected. If the lid was kept tightly clamped on the volcano the pressure under it would simply increase; but if it could be lifted by small degrees over a long period then the pressure might be gradually relieved until someday, perhaps, it would be safe to take the lid off altogether. This delicate and dangerous alternative, in which the West had every reason to wish them well, was the one the new Russian leaders adopted.

Beginning in the summer of 1953, and continuing through 1955, there was a general relaxation of economic impositions on the captive populations throughout East Europe. Then, in February 1956, came Khrushchev's notable address to the 20th Party Congress. In it he not only denounced Stalin and Stalinism, he denounced the rule of the secret police, and he called for greater individual liberty, as well as for a general liberalization of government to give greater scope to debate and to the intellectual and artistic life in general.

This address was eloquent testimony to the desire of the new leadership to break with the past. If there was any hope of doing this, it was only by such a bold, clean stroke of outspoken repudiation—whatever the cost. And the cost was immense, for it discredited the Soviet Union as leader of the world Communist movement by discrediting its conduct of that leadership for a generation past. It told the Communists the world over, who had been taught to accept Moscow's direction as infallible, that for some thirty years Moscow had misled them. It told them what sheep they (and the new Russian leaders themselves, as Stalin's former henchmen) had been. After this, how could anyone again give unquestioning obedience to Moscow's orders? How could anyone again accept its leadership?

In an earlier address at the 20th Congress Khrushchev had said that the main feature of the present era was "the emergence of socialism from the bounds of a single country and its transformation into a world system." The days of "socialism in one country" were over, for now there were many socialist countries. This was said as a boast, but in fact it constituted the prime dilemma of Moscow and the world Communist movement in the 1950's. No longer could Moscow hope to dictate to the other Communist parties and regimes. On April 17, 1956, the Cominform was dissolved by its members because, as they announced, it had "exhausted its function."

Palmiro Togliatti, the powerful leader of the Italian Communist Party, summed up the situation. "The Soviet model," he said, "cannot and must not any longer be obligatory. . . . The whole system becomes polycentric, and even in the Communist movement itself we cannot speak of a single guide but rather of a progress which is achieved by following paths that are often different." In other words, the one church must now split into many churches. "Polycentrism" was a euphemism for the fragmentation of the Communist movement.[2] Tito, who five years earlier had been the first great leader of a Communist movement to declare his independence of Moscow, and who had stood against it alone—Tito now had his triumph. Already the top leadership in Moscow had traveled to Belgrade, like the Holy Roman Emperor traveling to Canossa, and had publicly humbled itself before him, apologizing for the efforts Moscow had made under Stalin to compel his subservience.

Titoism, from now on, would become the rule in the Communist movement. The single ideological and political empire would never recover its credit. Everything was changed. The West no longer faced one mighty empire that seemed to be advancing inexorably toward world domination. Instead it now faced an empire that, in expanding, had fallen apart.

It would, however, be many years yet before the West would bring itself to recognize this, before it would begin to appreciate the implications of this triumph for Titoism. During that period it would continue to wage the Cold War along the old lines, as if nothing had happened, as if the time was still 1950.

.   .   .   .   .

To those who took the view that the Cold War was a contest between the good and the wicked for the mastery of the earth there could be no common ground between the two sides and the contest could end only with the total victory of one over the other. The objective of each side, in that case, must be to win it. On the other hand, if the purpose of the Cold War was simply to achieve a new international stability then both sides shared a common objective, which ought ultimately to provide a basis for agreement between them. They ought ultimately to be able to agree on terms, other than victory and defeat, by which each alike could expect to survive in reasonable security.

This difference in basic conception was fruitful of misunderstanding in Washington during the 1950's. Military men, especially, tended to feel that the Government should have a strategy for total victory in the Cold War, involving a calendar of projected offensives leading to it. Such a calendar, in the extreme form, would have a designated D-day on which the Western coalition would assume the strategic offensive against the enemy, and it would be completed by a V-day when the enemy power was finally broken. There would be a surrender scene and terms imposed by the victor. Others, recalling such historic struggles as the contest between Christendom and Islam, looked forward, rather, to a gradual resolution of the Cold War by the establishment, perhaps imperceptibly over a long period, of a stable equilibrium between the two sides, or by progressive shifts in the constellation of forces involving the gradual decentralization of power on both sides until there no longer were two sides. While the former were moved to intensify the Cold War (on Admiral Lord Fisher's principle that "moderation in war is imbecility"), the latter were moved

---

[2] The word is a contradiction in itself. How can anything have more than one center? "Polycentrism" is a euphemism for no center at all. Togliatti's statement may be found in Russian Institute, pp. 138–9.

to reduce its intensity toward the day when it should be no more, when men should ask one another what had ever become of it. In a convenient if slightly invidious verbal coinage, the former would come to be identified as "hards," the latter as "softs," and the public would read in the press of disputes between the two as particular issues of policy in the Cold War arose.

It was evident that the division between hards and softs existed no less in Moscow, where it tended to be equated with the distinction between those who still inclined toward Stalinism and those who had revolted from it.

These labels provide a convenient shorthand, although their application to individual persons, or in the context of particular issues, is at the risk of too crude a simplification. By his fundamental character as a mediator and a harmonizer of men President Eisenhower was clearly a soft. Secretary Dulles, on the other hand, as a man of Calvinistic disposition and an advocate, was clearly a hard. In Moscow, the relatively liberal Khrushchev was a soft, while Stalin's former confidant, Molotov, who continued as Foreign Minister until the summer of 1956, was a hard.

In a curious way, as the 1950's progressed the softs on the one side tended to become the tacit allies of the softs on the other, the hards on the one side of the hards on the other. This was because any indication of a soft policy on one side was bound to strengthen the position of the softs on the other, while hard behavior on one side strengthened the hards on the other by justifying them in their militancy.

This was exemplified in connection with the two abortive peace conferences, as we may call them, held at Geneva in 1955.

By the spring of 1955 great pressure had developed from many quarters for the convening of a "summit" conference, a conference of heads of government, to resolve the issue of the Cold War. The successor regime in Moscow had been pressing for such a conference in accordance with its ostensible efforts to relax international tensions and establish an international regime of what it called peaceful coexistence. This met with a ready response in Western public opinion, where there was a strong disposition to believe that if, instead of their representatives, the heads of government themselves sat around the table to talk out their differences, mutual understanding and an abatement of hostility would ensue. Consequently, in May arrangements were concluded to hold at Geneva in July a conference of the American, British, French, and Russian heads of government. Since such a conference, of four days' duration only, could not possibly settle the wide range of issues that presented themselves for resolution, it was intended simply as an opportunity for the heads of government to agree on the course to be followed in more detailed negotiations that would be opened by a longer conference of the four foreign ministers to follow.

To the softs on either side, whose objective was a settlement rather than victory, these two conferences presented a hopeful prospect. For those whose objective was victory they wore a different aspect. Mr. Eisenhower might well look hopefully toward the forthcoming conferences; but Mr. Dulles would not, since he could have no expectation that the diabolical Russian empire, which had been constantly growing in its strength, would surrender at them. (Similarly, we

may suppose that Messrs. Bulganin and Khrushchev[3] might be hopeful of the
détente at which they were aiming, while Mr. Molotov would be more impressed
with the unlikeliness of a Western surrender.)

There was reason for some hope of progress toward a general settlement on the
basis of peaceful coexistence, if that was the objective. Russia had just agreed to
withdraw from Austria, restoring the whole country to independence; it had
approached the Government of the Federal German Republic (which had just
joined NATO) in a move to establish normal relations with it; and it had
suddenly made very large concessions to the West in the general disarmament
negotiations that had for long been at a standstill. These moves, if not proof of
good faith, were tokens of it that could be disregarded neither by those who
wished for a settlement nor by those who, seeing no alternative to total victory,
did not.

Dulles, whose course was quite different in this from Eisenhower's, appeared
from the beginning to be trying to prevent any successful conferences from being
held by publicly establishing that the objective of such conferences would, in
effect, be Russian surrender. Immediately after the agreement to hold them he
told the press that the question of Russia's East European satellites might be
raised at them, and that the Russian concessions in Austria and in Yugoslavia
pointed toward similar Russian retreats in the rest of East Europe. This line,
which provoked a sharp reaction from Moscow, was bound to strengthen the
hand of those in Moscow who maintained that, since the West was seeking
nothing less than total victory, to make any concessions to it at all would be
dangerous.

The four days of the Geneva "summit" conference, at which Dulles and
Molotov remained in the background, brought no substantial agreement, but they
were not therefore without value. The fact that the principal spokesmen of East
and West dealt quietly, courteously, respectfully, and humanely with each other,
instead of shouting abuse at each other like primitive warriors about to enter
battle, was of the utmost importance. This marked an end to the unlimited
violence of language that the Russians had adopted in the fall of 1947, and that
had inevitably provoked some response in kind by the West, intensifying the
whole conflict.

When the four Foreign Ministers met in October it was clear that their
positions on the main issues did not allow of an agreed settlement. After the
Russian concessions on disarmament, the United States, for what may well be
considered sound reasons, had hardened its attitude, rejecting, now, disarmament
proposals that it had itself previously espoused. On the question of Germany,
which was the central issue between Russia and the West, it adhered to the
position, clearly unacceptable to Moscow, that Germany must be reunified on the
basis of terms that would allow it to belong to the Western camp after
reunification as before. Under the circumstances one may well conclude that in
1955 it was still too early to expect a solution of the central geographical and
strategical issues that, as the legacy of World War II, had engendered the Cold

---

[3] Bulganin, as Premier, was the head of the Russian Government, although Khrushchev,
as First Secretary of the Communist Party, was presumably more powerful and important.

War. The best that could be hoped for (and this was of prime importance) was the development of a tacit understanding that the continuing struggle between East and West would be conducted within limits of civility and moderation designed to prevent it from getting out of hand and ending in universal desolation.

An interesting by-play at the Foreign Ministers' Conference illustrates the implicit alliance between the hards (as between the softs) across the battlelines of the Cold War. After the first nine days of negotiation, during which Molotov, reflecting the new official attitude in Moscow, had appeared to be genuinely seeking an agreed settlement, the Conference adjourned for three days. Molotov took advantage of this break to return to Moscow, perhaps to seek instructions more to his liking. At the same time Dulles flew to Belgrade, where he indulged in the most provocative behavior possible. In a broadcast over the Belgrade radio, and in a statement made to the press after a meeting with Tito, he called for the liberation of Russia's East European satellites. Coming from the American Secretary of State, in Belgrade, and in the middle of the Geneva "peace" conference, nothing could have been better calculated to support the arguments of the hards in Moscow. At the end of the three days, when he left Moscow Airport for his return to Geneva, Molotov announced happily that he was returning with "new baggage." From that moment he was once more the old Molotov of Stalinist days who responded negatively and with abuse to every Western proposal. When the Conference ended in total failure some ten days later, the hards on both sides could take satisfaction in the fact that the slight mollification of the Cold War produced by the meeting between the heads of government had now been undone by the foreign ministers. There is a sense in which we may say that, at the Geneva Conferences of 1955, Dulles and Molotov defeated Eisenhower and Khrushchev.

The fact that from 1955 on the historian has to think in terms of this complex four-way relationship across the battlelines of the Cold War speaks for itself. Let no one believe, however, that as early as 1955 a substantial settlement of the intractable issues involved in the Cold War would have been possible if it had not been for the hards on either side.

seven
the "perils"
of khrushchev's
diplomacy,
1958-1960

ADAM B. ULAM

*Russian specialist Adam B. Ulam, a professor of
government at Harvard University, was born in Poland
in 1922 and received his Ph.D. from Harvard in 1947. He
is the author of* Titoism and the Cominform *(1952),*
The Unfinished Revolution *(1960),* The New Face
of Soviet Totalitarianism *(1963), and* The Bolsheviks
(1965). In the following selection from Expansion
and Coexistence: The History of Soviet Foreign Policy
1917–67 *(1968), Ulam analyzes the Cold War
from 1958 to 1960 from the perspective of the dilemmas
plaguing Russian Premier Nikita Khrushchev.
According to Ulam, China's incipient split from Russia
forced Khrushchev to seek a settlement of the German
issue, a goal he pursued by a combination of bellicose and
conciliatory policies. Ulam's treatment of the 1958–60
period triggers some important questions: How
accurately did the United States perceive Russian
interests and motives? How effectively did the United
States respond to the overtures for coexistence?
Was another opportunity for reduction of tensions
missed?*

Source: Adam B. Ulam, *Expansion and Coexistence: The History
of Soviet Foreign Policy, 1917–67* (New York: Frederick A.
Praeger, 1968), pp. 613, 619–34. Reprinted by permission
of the publisher.

Beginning in 1957–58, Soviet foreign policy was increasingly dominated by the triangular relation between the United States, China, and the U.S.S.R. To put it in plain language, the Soviets found themselves under pressure to reassert the policies of coexistence so as to minimize the chances of nuclear conflict, and at the same time forced to conduct expansionist policies so as to prevent an open break with China. Not that the latter policies can be explained purely in terms of Chinese pressures, for as we have seen they also relate to ideological dilemmas within the U.S.S.R. Also, not insignificantly, the disarray of Western policies, especially concerning non-European areas, created an almost irresistible temptation for the U.S.S.R. to try to score points. The dazzling succession of opportunities presented in the Middle East and later on in Africa undoubtedly would have tempted the Soviet policy-makers even had there been no Communist China.

. . . . .

Paradoxical as it must appear, the growing trouble with China was to precipitate the Khrushchev regime into another crisis with the West. The most basic issue in Europe, that of Germany, had to be solved. And the greatest Soviet fear—of West Germany acquiring atomic weapons—had to be removed before the "unshakable unity" of the socialist camp was exposed as something less than that. There were also sound secondary reasons for what became the "Berlin crisis": the perennial need of Khrushchev and the Soviet regime to score successes in foreign policy; the need to close off West Berlin, a gaping wound in the flank of the German Democratic Republic, the main gate through which hundreds of thousands of East Germans sought their way to the freedom and prosperity of the West. And the timing of the Berlin crisis leaves no doubt as to the wider context in which the Soviets made their move, nor, even more forcibly, does the fact that the Soviet note to the Western Powers of November 27 which opened the crisis was followed on December 21 by an official Chinese statement from Peking endorsing it. The Soviets were going to squeeze the last ounce of benefit from their fast-waning alliance with China. The latter, for her own reasons, welcomed any new confrontation between the United States and the U.S.S.R. and was willing to comply.

The Soviet note was of an unusual length, but the gist was simple. Thirteen years had passed since the war, but the situation in Germany was still abnormal. The U.S.S.R. recognized that, lamentably, two German states had come into existence instead of one. But the Western Powers must also recognize this fact. One remaining abnormality was the status of West Berlin and its continuing occupation. It should be terminated. The U.S.S.R. was quite willing to have West Berlin be a free demilitarized city. It proposed *for the next six months* to make no alteration in Western access to the city. But if no agreement was forthcoming in that period of time then the Soviet Union would turn East Berlin over to the East Germans and sign with them an agreement renouncing any vestiges of her occupation powers. It would thus be up to East Germany to negotiate with the three Western Powers as to their rights of access to West Berlin, and East Germany would have full right to ban the Western Powers' communications across its territory. Any attack on East Germany would, of course, be regarded by all the signatories of the Warsaw Pact as an attack upon them.

On the face of it, the Soviet note was but another in a long series of threats and pressures exerted upon the West. But this time there was also the air of an ultimatum: recognize East Germany within six months or get out of Berlin, the Western Powers were told. If they refused to do either, they faced the probability of East Germany barring their access to Berlin, and any attempt to break this new blockade (and the implication was clear that it would also extend to air traffic) would mean war with the U.S.S.R. To anybody familiar with the dominant voice in Western diplomacy, that of ailing Dulles, it was obvious what the *immediate* Western reaction would be: this was but another Soviet exercise in blackmail. To be sure, the American attitude later softened, largely in answer to British pleas to explore what the Soviets had in mind, but that the United States would agree to recognize East Germany or clear out of Berlin was inconceivable.

What, in fact, *were* the Russian motives? To us *now,* it is clear that the main Soviet objective was to secure an agreement that would make it impossible for West Germany to obtain nuclear weapons. This was indicated in the Soviet note, which said that "the best way to solve the Berlin question . . . would mean the withdrawal of the Federal German Republic from NATO, with the simultaneous withdrawal of the German Democratic Republic from the Warsaw Treaty Organization. . . . Neither of the two German states would have any armed forces in excess of those needed to maintain law and order at home and to guard their frontier." The Soviets thought that pressure on Berlin was the most efficacious way of obtaining what they really wanted, the neutralization of Germany, and one suspects that for the moment they would have settled for a firm pledge that West Germany would be barred from being a nuclear force.

But Khrushchev might have pondered the tale of the little boy who used to alarm his elders by exclaiming that he was drowning, eventually lost his "credibility," and was allowed to drown. He had threatened with rockets and bombs over Suez, over the landings in Lebanon and Jordan, and now over Berlin. How could one tell in which case he considered the issue to be one of national security for the U.S.S.R. and in which he was bluffing? Even for a person without Dulles' rigorous moralistic and legalistic attitude, it would have been impossible to tell that on the German issue the Russians were deeply in earnest and not just eager to score another triumph. Not being mind-readers and not having an agent in the highest Kremlin circles, the Western statesmen were likewise unable then to deduce that in setting a time limit, the Soviet leaders were influenced by the widening split with China: in a year or two this increasingly violent controversy might become public knowledge, in which case their bargaining powers vis-à-vis the United States would be seriously reduced.

In addition to this complicated design of Soviet fears and hopes, one receives the impression of clashing tendencies within the Khrushchev regime which did not allow him a completely free hand either in foreign or in domestic affairs. The special Twenty-first Party Congress summoned with great fanfare for January 1959, apart from confirming the new seven-year economic plan, failed to make any dramatic decisions, and one suspects that some of the original plans for the Congress had to be canceled because of a division among the leaders. And there were interesting undertones in the foreign-policy part of Khrushchev's speech at the Congress. First of all, he put stronger emphasis than ever before on the absolute inadmissibility of war in the nuclear age and made warm references to the United States and the need for an East-West *détente*. But the crucial sentence—it is one of the few that is underlined in the official text—was: *"One can and must construct in the Far East and the whole Pacific Ocean area a zone of peace and, first of all, a zone free of atomic weapons."* This supremely important passage, the most open expression thus far of the Soviet hope that somehow Communist China might be prevented from ever acquiring atomic weapons, was overlooked in the West, in contrast to Khrushchev's threats and taunts[1] about West Germany.

In view of this proposal, and Khrushchev's fervent affirmation of the Soviet desire for peaceful coexistence and an end to the cold war, how did the Soviets manage to get (for the last time!) a cordial endorsement of their policies from Chou En-lai (present at the Congress) and, in a special message, from Mao himself, who stressed once more the "unshakable unity of the socialist camp"? The explanation is provided by a Russo-Chinese announcement of February 9, 1959, of the most extensive Soviet economic and technological aid thus far to Communist China—5 billion rubles' worth of Soviet services and goods, mostly in heavy industry, to be provided during the next seven years. In addition, Chinese experts were to be trained in the U.S.S.R. and more Soviet technicians were to be sent to China. The "unshakable unity of the socialist camp" was becoming increasingly expensive.

This agreement with China, plus what he undoubtedly considered as Western obtuseness, largely accounts for Khrushchev's erratic and irritable behavior during the months between the Twenty-first Congress and his trip to the United States in September 1959. He needed a success in Germany because he undoubtedly felt this would strengthen his position at home and within the Communist camp. It might, he probably felt, still enable him to impose the Soviet viewpoint and Soviet caution on the Chinese Communists, then in the midst of serious economic troubles. Yet the West was refusing his (by his lights) perfectly reasonable proposals on Germany while remaining oblivious to the real danger: China's eventual emancipation from Soviet influence and her acquisition of nuclear weapons. . . .

The First Secretary's bad humor erupted during Prime Minister Macmillan's visit to Moscow in February 1959. Britain was known to be the Western nation most eager for a summit meeting, British public opinion most ready to accept some form of a compromise solution on Germany. But in view of the American and French reservations, all that Macmillan could propose was yet another foreign ministers' meeting of the Big Four. To Khrushchev, who hoped for a breakthrough on the German question and who had hopes that a summit meeting would take up a larger agenda, this was insufferable, and he was rude to his

---

[1] A typical Khrushchevism: Chancellor Adenauer is a believing Christian; he should consequently worry about his soul, for surely for his policies he will go straight to hell!

British guest.[2] But before Macmillan departed, he grudgingly agreed to a foreign ministers' conference and indicated that his deadline on Berlin need not be taken too literally.

The conference of foreign ministers of Britain, the United States, France, and the U.S.S.R. which met in Geneva followed the melancholy pattern of such previous meetings: it was long (two sessions, May 11–June 20 and July 13–August 20) and inconclusive. The British were eager for a compromise. The French, with General de Gaulle now in power, were already suspicious of anything which might smack of a deal between the "Anglo-Saxons" and the Russians. The United States' position (Dulles was now out of the picture) was more amenable to the British viewpoint, but, by the same token, she was not, in view of Chancellor Adenauer's warnings, going to agree to anything which smacked of recognition of East Germany. The Soviet position on the "two Germanies" was unyielding, but Gromyko was flexible on the time limit, indicating that negotiations could take a year or a year and a half before the U.S.S.R. would feel compelled to act unilaterally on a peace treaty with East Germany. The Soviets, in brief, wanted a summit meeting and were not going to agree to a binding solution anywhere else.

In fact we now know that the attention of the Soviet leaders during those summer months was centered on events elsewhere. A violent secret dispute was taking place between the leaders of the Soviet and Chinese Communist parties. The later Chinese version of this dispute is quite pat, as we have seen, consisting in an allegation that in June 1959 the Soviet government went back on its 1957 agreement to provide China with atomic "know-how" and a "sample" atom bomb. The Soviet answer to this charge, made in 1963, implies very strongly that the Soviet government had wanted in 1959 to be empowered to pledge that China would refrain from the production of nuclear weapons *if* for her part the United States would make a similar pledge about West Germany. And this was in fact to be Khrushchev's ace argument at the forthcoming summit conference: accept my proposal for two neutralized Germanies, and we shall guarantee that China will not produce nuclear weapons. It is not difficult to reconstruct Khrushchev's argument to the Chinese: Why, especially in view of the deplorable state of your economy, do you sink your resources into this expensive business of making atom bombs? The U.S.S.R. has made it clear that she would consider any nuclear attack upon China as an attack upon herself? But this argument evidently found no favor with Mao. Was it convincing to some other Chinese leaders? A very important meeting of the Central Committee of the CCP took place in Lushan in July and August 1959, at which much of the anti-Mao opposition was evidently crushed. Marshal Peng Teh-huai, Minister of Defense, and some other high officials were dismissed. Had they been in favor of accepting the Soviet proposals? Or, as was hinted later (in 1966 and 1967), were they at the prompting of the Russians even attempting to remove Mao and his group? We have no way of knowing. We simply know that a new and decisive turn was

---

[2] The foreign ministers could never settle anything since they did not have the power that only heads of governments possessed, said Khrushchev. In a colorful illustration of this, he explained that were he to ask his foreign minister to take off his trousers and sit on a block of ice Gromyko would have to comply.

taken at that time in Sino-Soviet relations and that from then on neither Khrushchev nor any Soviet leader was able to speak for China.

Awareness of this fact soured what otherwise would have been the crowning point of Khrushchev's career, his visit to the bastion of capitalism. Freed from Dulles' tutelage, President Eisenhower was eager to have the mercurial Soviet statesman visit the United States, despite the misgivings of personages as diverse as Adenauer and Cardinal Spellman: Chairman Khrushchev, as the official American term had it, thus referring to the *less* important of his two jobs, would be able to see for himself the peaceful, friendly ways of the Americans, he would be able to disabuse himself of the Marxian stereotypes about capitalism, etc.

For his part, Khrushchev considered the invitation a personal triumph. He was the first head of the Russian government to visit the United States: the Tsars wouldn't, and his incomparably more powerful predecessor couldn't. Apart from his love of travel, there was the undoubted fact that the trip would raise his standing at home (if not in Peking) : in the nuclear age even social amenities between the heads of the two super-powers took on the appearance of political acts and tended to be reassuring. In the rather amusing account of the visit compiled by his journalist son-in-law Alexei Adzhubei, this theme is somewhat pompously spelled out: "The head of the Soviet government, accepting the invitation, went overseas not as a private person . . . but as head of the government of one great power to meet the head of another. . . . Behind him there stood the 200 million people of the first socialist country in the world and more than that the whole socialist camp with its billion people."

As to the substantive results of the visit, Khrushchev could be under few illusions. The late Mr. Dulles, despite or perhaps because of his inflexibility, enjoyed a certain respect in Soviet official circles, as, one would think, a kind of American Molotov. But the Russians, as Khrushchev's actions were to indicate in 1960, despite their undoubted esteem for his human qualities did not consider President Eisenhower to possess a firm grasp on the realities of the world situation or to be capable of initiating a new bold line of policy. Most important of all, Khrushchev's freedom of operation was by now severely limited by his quarrel with China. Peking was seething with rage, first at the very fact of the visit, and secondly at the official Soviet communiqué issued on September 9 on the occasion of the flare-up between Chinese and Indian troops on the Himalayan border, which urged both countries to be reasonable, refused to support the Chinese side, and, to Peking in its current frame of mind, lent substance to the worst suspicions about the purport of Khrushchev's visit to America.

Thus Khrushchev was unable to bargain for an atom-free zone in Asia against a similar one in Germany. The most that he could now expect from the visit was an American agreement to have a summit meeting, and a careful exploration of the possibility of drawing the United States away from her unyielding position on Germany.

As an exercise in public relations, the visit, which began on September 15 and went on two weeks, was an imposing affair. Nikita Sergeievich traveled with a suite that would have been thought excessive for a Tsar; one can understand the presence of the foreign minister, members of Khrushchev's family, and a bevy of Soviet newspapermen, but there were also physicists, medical authorities, and, most surprising of all, Khrushchev's (and Stalin's) favorite author, Sholokhov. Theatricalities filled the American and Soviet press: Khrushchev sparring with newspapermen, indignant about the refusal (for security reasons) to let him visit Disneyland, shocked by the levity of a Hollywood movie, extolling his favorite crop, corn, on a visit to an Iowa farm, everywhere proclaiming the virtues of coexistence. In the Soviet versions, each appearance was a personal triumph: "simple Americans" came to realize how Communism and its great leader had been misrepresented to them, malicious interviewers were confounded by calm and incisive replies, everybody agreed that never had such an impressive foreign statesman visited the United States. With the Americans, the greatest hit was Mme. Khrushchev, whose dignity and affability made up for the often boorish behavior of her husband.

The latter brought to the United States, in addition to his suite, an enormous chip on his shoulder. Any Russian was liable to be irritated by Eisenhower's well-meaning but insensitive hints about American affluence, but Nikita Sergeievich reacted to them with absurdities: no, the average citizen of the U.S.S.R. did not long for a house of his own, he preferred an apartment; he abhorred the notion of a private automobile, being quite satisfied with public transportation. The Soviet leader could not help openly taunting Vice President Nixon, with whom he had had a run-in before at an American exhibition in Moscow. It had been stipulated that Khrushchev was to be treated like a head of state, but he lacked both the awesome dignity of Stalin and the suppleness of a lesser official like Mikoyan, and the occasional impetuousness and boorishness he revealed in America was to be a factor in his eventual downfall.

In his account of the visit, Eisenhower has the following passage, which unwittingly explains perhaps some of his guest's irritation:

Referring to Red China, Khrushchev said that he had some personal viewpoints about our attitude towards that nation. He asked if I would like to discuss the subject. I answered that I thought there was little use to do so, for the simple reason that Red China had put herself beyond the pale so far as the United States was concerned. . . . He took my refusal in good part and implied that he had been specifically asked to bring up the subject with me, by whom, he did not say. He did add, however, that allegations of differences between the Soviets and Red China . . . were ridiculous by their very nature. He and Mao Tse-tung were good friends; the two nations, he said, would always stand together in any international dispute.

The President's refusal to discuss what was, after all, the most important international problem facing the two countries, Berlin or no Berlin, could be taken as a sign either of American obtuseness or of extreme cleverness (having gotten wind of the dispute, the Americans did not propose to tip their hand). Alas, there is no doubt which it was. Later on, Khrushchev was to credit himself with additional delicacy on this occasion. In the intimate atmosphere of Camp David, the President's retreat, he had felt like asking Eisenhower why he was allowing U-2 flights over the U.S.S.R., but it would have been too embarrassing.

Whatever Khrushchev's real reasons for not mentioning this subject and for not opening his heart about his troubles with China, it is likely that he had concluded that neither jarring questions nor excessive frankness would be conducive to the aim uppermost in his mind: a summit conference. To this end, Khrushchev modified his position on the Berlin-Germany settlement and accepted that, while negotiations could not be prolonged indefinitely, there should be no fixed time limit on them. In other words, the element of ultimatum was removed from the Soviet position, and with this difficulty out of the way President Eisenhower agreed to a summit meeting later on in the year. In 1960, he was supposed to return Khrushchev's visit and become the first head of the American government to visit Russia. These two agreements lent an air of cordiality to the final phase of the Soviet-American talks; "the spirit of Camp David," as it became known, seemed to promise some form of settlement of the German issue, a decisive East-West *détente,* and perhaps even more.

Soon practical difficulties were to interfere with the time-table of the *rapprochement.* In two Western capitals, Bonn and Paris, the spirit of Camp David was viewed with suspicion. To Adenauer, the American-British position was not firm enough; a Big Four meeting might result in at least partial capitulation by the West on the question of recognition of East Germany. For his part, General de Gaulle was already apprehensive of a possible "deal" between the United States and the U.S.S.R. by which the two super-powers would establish a dual hegemony in the world. It was largely in answer to his objections that the summit meeting was postponed until the next May. By that time, Eisenhower's ability to enter into a binding agreement with the U.S.S.R. would be restricted in view of the approaching presidential elections, and French pride could be appeased by Khrushchev coming to visit France *before* the summit meeting. Most of all, de Gaulle counted on something happening before the summit meeting that would prevent the United States and the U.S.S.R. from reaching a comprehensive agreement, that would preclude France's playing the role for which she was so eager—of a Great Power dominating Western Europe. And, to be sure, "something" did happen.

For the Soviets the delay was an inconvenience. Time was running out; the Soviets could not long prevent disclosure of their disagreements with China and, thus, a weakening of their bargaining position. And Khrushchev needed visible successes to bolster up his position at home. On his return to Moscow, he was given (or, properly speaking, gave himself) a triumphant reception, on which occasion he hailed Eisenhower as a constructive statesman and confirmed his invitation to Russia. (He must have known how uncertain was the current direction of American policy, how West German objections and French pressures were likely to strengthen the case against reaching an agreement with the Soviets—hence the quite open flattery of the American President.) But almost immediately he had to go on a less congenial trip to Peking.

General de Gaulle's objections to a summit conference were undoubtedly dwarfed by the Chinese Communists'. Four years later, this is what they had to say: "Back from the Camp David talks, [Khrushchev] went so far as to try to sell China the U. S. plot of the 'two Chinas' and, at the state banquet celebrating the Tenth Anniversary of the Founding of the People's Republic

of China, he read China a lecture against 'testing by force the stability of
the capitalist system.' " As usual the Chinese interpretation is probably too
drastic. Khrushchev must have attempted to appease the rising Chinese anger
by pointing out that a Soviet success in Germany could not but strengthen the
position of the socialist camp as a whole, that Russia would then be able to
press more energetically on behalf of Chinese interests in Formosa, etc. In
the speech in question, he took great pains to soothe the Chinese fears of
Soviet appeasement. What entreaties or even threats Khrushchev employed
we do not know. But for the moment he succeeded in preventing an open break
and in preserving the veneer of that great friendship with Mao Tse-tung
about which he had so fervently assured Eisenhower. On their part, the Chinese
leaders were most likely to count, as did de Gaulle, on a development that
would wreck the prospects of Soviet-American *rapprochement*. Until the
summit meeting was actually to materialize and bear fruit, they would hold
their fire.

   The evidence presented above suggests very strongly that the diplomatic
maneuvers executed by Khrushchev in 1958–59 were part of a grand design
through which he hoped to effect at least a partial solution of the German
problem as well as to prevent or considerably delay the Chinese acquisition
of atomic weapons. Some tantalizing questions still remain. What would have
happened had there been a more perceptive appraisal in Washington of
Soviet problems and aspirations? What if a summit conference had taken place
in December 1959? There were voices in the West (among them,
paradoxically, General de Gaulle's) that recognized the multitude of Russia's
problems, principally that concerning China. But while viewing the Sino-Soviet
problem in apocalyptic long-range terms, the West ignored how intense
the conflict already was, and that a *united* and *prompt* initiative might affect it.
But it is doubtful that, even had Khrushchev unburdened himself to Eisenhower,
the lackadaisical course of American policy would have changed. Bold
improvisations were not in its style. It is equally doubtful that, China's
precarious economic position (undoubtedly a factor in his calculations)
notwithstanding, Khruschchev could have subordinated Chinese foreign policy
to Soviet interests. Still, on the Western side no attempt was made to explore
this whole problem.
   There can be no question that this grand design represented also a very
personal commitment on Khrushchev's part. He was going to pass into history
as a man who secured a long-term *détente* in the cold war, a lengthy period
of peace for the development of his people's economy and well-being.

.   .   .   .   .

   In the course of 1960, two elements in Khrushchev's juggling act came
crashing to the ground. The Soviet Union's now intense conflict with China
became public knowledge, first in the Communist world and then in the
West. Coincidental with this, but not unconnected, came the collapse of the
summit meeting and of any hope of solving the German issue through

negotiations. The remaining years of Khrushchev's rule were to bring dangerous confrontations with the United States over Berlin and Cuba and then an amelioration in Soviet-American relations with the relief felt over the peaceful resolution of the Cuban missile crisis. But the latter in turn contributed to the intensification of Russia's quarrel with China and then public disclosure of its main points.

. . . . .

In the spring of 1960 the Soviet grand design lay all but shattered, and it was inconceivable that the results of any summit conference could make it feasible in the future. The Chinese attitude on the subject must have been made clear to Khrushchev on his visit to Peking in 1959, but just to make sure that the Russians labored under no illusions, the Peking leaders fired their heaviest salvo thus far as the conference approached. On April 16, 1960, *Red Flag,* a Peking journal, published "Long Live Leninism!," an article whose authorship was subsequently attributed to Mao himself. The article did not attack Khrushchev and the Soviets in so many words, but opprobrious references to Yugoslav Communists and assorted revisionists were transparent enough. The involved semantics and esoteric allusions amounted to a public warning: if you Russians push *détente* with the West one step further, we shall denounce you by name as being as vile as the Yugoslav revisionists. As for any schemes for limiting the spread of nuclear armaments at their expense, the Chinese were not buying. They were not afraid of an atomic war:

We consistently oppose the launching of criminal wars by imperialism.
. . . But should the imperialists impose such sacrifices on the peoples
of various countries, we believe that, just as the experience of the
Russian revolution and the Chinese revolution shows, those
sacrifices would be repaid on the debris of a dead imperialism. The
victorious people would create very swiftly a civilization thousands of
times higher than the capitalist system and a truly beautiful system
for themselves.

The last sentence, as was to become clear some years later, left the Soviet leaders breathless. They overlooked the fact (proof of how lacking they were in introspection) that it came close to what Khrushchev himself had said on several occasions; now the Chinese were saying that socialism would survive a nuclear war—why, it would flourish better than before! It was one thing, though, for the Soviets to frighten the capitalists with such supposed equanimity about an atomic holocaust. But for Chinese Communists to express such sentiments seriously for the benefit of fellow-Communists! . . .

One-half of the grand design was thus completely lost. Khrushchev would go to the summit without any possibility of producing a dramatic proposal to prohibit nuclear weapons in the Pacific area in return for a similar prohibition in Germany. What was left was the increasingly dim prospect of securing one-sided concessions from the West. There was little that the Soviet

government could offer in exchange. The time had passed when the East
German state could be considered expendable. The threat of arming
East Germany with nuclear weapons was likely to petrify the Poles and the
Czechs, if not indeed the Russians themselves. After a while, it was wisely
decided to discard this gambit as a bargaining weapon. What, then, was left?
Khrushchev's hopes were obviously based on Eisenhower's incautious
admission at Camp David that the situation in Berlin was "abnormal" and
on the well-known British eagerness to secure a Berlin agreement that would
relieve the anxiety about a possible clash there.

For their part, the responsible American officials approached the prospect
of the summit conference in the spirit of a young girl being asked out for
the evening by a well-known seducer, previous encounters with whom had led
to scandalous propositions rather than honorable declarations. Whether there
was some nervousness in the State Department as to what the President
might say while in a private meeting with Khrushchev, with Macmillan
whispering his entreaties, or whether they wanted to warn the American
public against excessive hopes, Secretary of State Christian Herter and
Under Secretary C. Douglas Dillon proceeded to adopt an unyielding attitude
in public speeches. The latter, in a speech of April 20, spoke in terms
calculated to raise the temperature of the already sorely tried Khrushchev:
"Is the Soviet Union prepared to remove its forces from East Germany and the
Eastern European countries on which they are imposed? Is it willing to grant
self-determination to the East Germans and the peoples of the Soviet-dominated
states in Eastern Europe . . . abandon the fiction of a separate North
Korea . . . ?" The answer to all those questions was obviously no, or, rather,
if Khrushchev had chosen to be painfully frank, he could have explained
that it was not within his power to do these things, that, alas, they confused
his powers with Stalin's. In Baku on April 25, the Soviet leader wondered
plaintively:

*Why then did Dillon have to make a statement so obviously out of
tune with the tenor of relations between the U.S.S.R. and the United
States since my conversations with President Eisenhower at Camp
David? Perhaps this is no more than a manifestation of the pugnacity
of a diplomat who has taken into his head that some pressure on the
other side before the talks might make it more compliant. . . .
Some people apparently hope to reduce this meeting to an ineffectual
exchange of opinion and pleasant—it may be—talks.*

Khrushchev repeated that concrete progress must be made at the summit
meeting on two issues: disarmament and a peace treaty with Germany.
Otherwise, and he was now more emphatic than before, the U.S.S.R. would
go ahead with her own treaty with East Germany; and then—on this also
he was more emphatic than before—the West would lose its rights of access
to West Berlin by "land, water, and air."

This speech did not mark, as has sometimes been asserted, Khrushchev's
abandonment of hopes for the summit. It marked his growing

pessimism—justified, in view of Herter's and Dillon's speeches—that the Soviets would not get their way, and an escalation of his psychological pressure on the West. (It was interesting that he distinguished between Eisenhower and the State Department, implying that the latter was not in line with the President's conciliatory position.)

The celebrated U-2 incident began on May 1 with the downing of an American spy plane deep within the territory of the U.S.S.R. and the imprisonment of its pilot. (Such flights had been taking place since 1956. While the Russians had had no reason to be enchanted with the Americans flying over their territory and were undoubtedly irritated by their inability to bring the high-altitude planes down, it is reasonable to assume that they had accepted the flights as an unpleasant fact of international life.) On May 5, in a dramatic speech to the Supreme Soviet, Khrushchev announced the downing of the plane but chose to withhold the fact that the pilot, with his photographic equipment, had been captured. After the State Department issued a feeble communiqué about the pilot having probably lost consciousness and the automatic pilot bringing the "weather research plane" down into the heart of the U.S.S.R., Khrushchev with some delight revealed that the Soviets were holding the American flier and the evidence proving the real purpose of the flight. Caught red-handed, the State Department chose on May 7 and 9 to reveal the full extent of previous American penetrations of Soviet air space, to defend and justify this record, and to associate the President with the decision to employ this form of spying. This was to compound the original error of answering the first Soviet announcement: it was unprecedented in diplomatic history for a government to admit responsibility for spying publicly, and incredible that a head of state should be drawn into this admission.

Khrushchev's actions are still difficult to analyze. But it is entirely conceivable that his statements of May 5 and 7 were prompted by the belief that discomfiture would make the Americans more pliable, that something might be rescued from the summit meeting after all. But Eisenhower's incredible assumption of the responsibility for the flights made his anger, feigned in the beginning, very real. We do not know whether there had been any voices in the Soviet leadership who had expressed skepticism about Khrushchev's summit tactics, or his invitation to Eisenhower, or his apparent belief that the President could shake off the objections of Adenauer and the State Department and strike a bargain over Germany. But Khrushchev had committed himself when he presented Eisenhower to the Soviet people as a man of "wise statesmanship . . . courage and will power." Now he was made to look ridiculous, if not to the Russian people, who were accustomed and somewhat indifferent to drastic shifts in official evaluations of foreign statesmen, then to his colleagues. And it was not difficult to imagine the reaction in Peking! Khrushchev's subsequent course of action suggests considerable personal vindictiveness toward the President and an attempt to embarrass his party in the approaching presidential elections.

In Paris, where he arrived on May 14, Khrushchev continued his theatricalities: unless Eisenhower apologized, promised to discontinue the flights, and punished those responsible for them, the Soviet government would walk out of the conference. Since the President obviously could not apologize (he did indicate that the overflights would be stopped), especially in view of Khrushchev's insulting tone, the summit conference was aborted. Khrushchev rubbed salt into the wound by suggesting that a new gathering take place in six or eight months—i.e., after the new president was installed—and he withdrew his invitation to Eisenhower to visit Russia.

After some further antics at a press conference, Khrushchev flew to Berlin. The world held its breath, expecting a treaty to be signed between the U.S.S.R. and East Germany and an immediate challenge to Western rights in Berlin. In fact, Khrushchev simply repeated his suggestion for another, later summit meeting and recommended that in the meantime neither side take unilateral action on Germany. The immediate fears of a cataclysmic clash—sufficiently great for the Secretary of Defense to order a world-wide alert of American forces—were for the moment appeased.

There were naturally many conjectures in the West about the reasons for the break-up of the summit conference. Was Khrushchev's anger real, or was it simulated in order to provide a pretext for breaking up a meeting at which the Soviets were unlikely to secure any gains? This question has already been discussed. Were his hands in some sense tied by "pro-Chinese members of the Presidium," as the phrase went? This is a most unlikely conjecture. Khrushchev most probably had come under more severe internal criticism for his original promise in 1957 to help China with nuclear development than for his subsequent backing down on that agreement. With their intense nationalist orientation, who among the Soviet leaders would seek a road to power by endorsing the Chinese viewpoint, against Russian interests? In 1961 Molotov was accused by implication of connections with Peking, but this was simply a modern variant of such accusations as those in the 1930's that Trotsky and Bukharin worked for British Intelligence. Khrushchev was undoubtedly on the spot simply because his schemes had not worked and he was getting into more and more trouble with the West and with the Chinese.

eight

kennedy: from cold warrior to advocate of coexistence

WILLIAM G. CARLETON

In an article in the Antioch Review, *written shortly after President Kennedy's assassination, William G. Carleton, emeritus professor of political science at the University of Florida, provided an early assessment of the Kennedy administration. Carleton's interpretation that Kennedy only belatedly pursued coexistence has found acceptance in many subsequent works. Carleton is representative of many scholars who believe that the containment policy of 1947 was necessary, but that the United States was not sufficiently responsive to subsequent opportunities to reduce Cold War tensions. Carleton was born in 1903 and educated at Indiana University and the University of Florida, where he then taught for forty years. In addition to his several articles on American diplomacy in the Cold War era, Carleton also wrote* The Revolution in American Foreign Policy *(1963), a comprehensive history of American diplomacy since World War II. Considering Carleton's essay in the context of the preceding selections by Halle and Ulam, did the Kennedy administration bring about any significant change in American policy?*

Source: William G. Carleton, "Kennedy in History: An Early Appraisal," *Antioch Review* 24 (Fall 1964): 289–96. Reprinted by permission of the publisher.

In foreign policy, the first two years of Kennedy were ambiguous. In the third year, there was a clearer sense of direction, one which promised to harmonize American policy with emerging new realities in the world.

At the time of the Kennedy accession, the postwar world was disintegrating. Bipolarization was giving way to depolarization. The Sino-Soviet rift was widening. With the single exception of little Vietminh, all the old European colonies that had recently gained their independence had escaped Communism, although there were Communist guerrilla activities in some of them. The trend was to a new pluralism, a new diversity. The nuclear revolution in war and the American-Soviet nuclear deterrents had rendered an ultimate military showdown unthinkable. The United States was ahead in the nuclear arms race.

In Europe, despite Khrushchev's bluster about West Berlin, the existing arrangements in East and Central Europe were ripening into a more overt *modus vivendi,* by way of tacit understanding rather than formal political agreements. Trade and intercourse between East and West Europe were increasing, the satellites were operating more independently of Moscow, and an all-European economic and cultural co-operation seemed slowly to be replacing the postwar's clear-cut division between the "two Europes." West Europeans were becoming less interested in NATO because they were more and more convinced that there would be no Soviet military aggression in Europe, due to the nuclear deterrent and other reasons. The drive to West European political integration was slackening, owing to the decline of external pressures and to De Gaulle's opposition to the supranational approach. Forces within the Six, composing the Common Market, were honestly divided over whether they wanted an inward-looking European community or an outward-looking Atlantic one.

In short, Kennedy was confronted with a new fluidity, a necessity and an opportunity for a reappraisal of American foreign policy. How much of the old foreign policy was still applicable? What aspects required a new orientation? To what degree was it safe, realistic, and advantageous to strike out in new directions? In some ways this ambiguous situation was more agonizing to decision makers than the obvious crisis situation with which Truman and Acheson had had to deal in the late 1940's and early 1950's. It is no wonder that some aspects of the Kennedy record in foreign affairs seem somewhat confused, even contradictory.

The chief stumbling block to an American-Soviet *détente* continued to be Berlin, the two Germanies, and the territorial arrangements in East and Central Europe. Kennedy rejected explorations of a definitive settlement, and if in the future a genuine American-Soviet *rapprochement* develops, this rejection is likely to be held against him. However, he did move informally in the direction of a more openly tacit recognition of the existing arrangements in East and Central Europe. He deferred less to Adenauer's views than previous administrations had done. In his interview in *Izvestia,* remarkable for its clarity and candor, he agreed that it would not be advisable to let West Germany have its own nuclear weapons. After the Communists built the Berlin Wall, Kennedy resisted all pressures to use force to tear it down.

Nevertheless, during his first two years in office, Kennedy seems needlessly to have fanned the tensions of the dying Cold War. (It may be that "needlessly" is too strong a word; perhaps Kennedy thought he needed to arouse the country to obtain a more balanced military program, more foreign economic aid, the Alliance for Progress; perhaps he thought, too, that a truculent tone was necessary to convince Khrushchev that America would stand firm under duress for its rights in Berlin.) His inaugural address was alarmist, already historically off key, more suited to the Stalinist era than to 1961. His first State of the Union Message was even more alarmist. The nation was told that the world tide was unfavorable, that each day we were drawing near the maximum danger. His backing of the Cuban invasion in April, 1961, further fanned the Cold War. His statement to newspaper publishers and editors gathered at the White House in May—that the United States was in the most critical period of its history—increased the popular anxieties. He over-reacted to Khrushchev's Vienna ultimatum in June, for in recent years Khrushchev's repeated deadlines and backdowns over West Berlin had become a kind of pattern. But for Kennedy, Vienna seems to have been a traumatic experience. On his return home he appealed to Americans to build do-it-yourself bomb shelters, and this produced a war psychology in the country and all manner of frenetic behavior, caused right-wingism to soar (1961 was the year the membership and financial "take" of the right-wing organizations reached their peak), and weakened confidence abroad in Kennedy's judgment.

There are no defenders of the Cuban fiasco of April, 1961. Even had the expedition of the Cuban exiles been given American naval and air support and forced a landing, there is scant evidence that the Cubans, at that time devoted to Castro, would have revolted en masse and welcomed the invaders as deliverers. More likely a nasty civil war would have followed, with the Americans, giving increasing support to the invaders, cast in the role of subjugators. The C.I.A. had already rejected the social-revolutionary leadership of the anti-Castro Manuel Rey for a non-leftist leadership, and this would have made the task of overthrowing Castro even more difficult. The world would have looked on with dismay, and outside the United States the whole affair would have come to be regarded as "another Hungary." It is ironical that Kennedy, the generalist with a critical intelligence, the politician with a feel for popular moods, should on this occasion have been taken in by the bureaucrats and the "experts." Prodded by his own anti-Castro stand during the election campaign, Kennedy must have wanted desperately to believe in the reliability of those dossiers of the intelligence agents.

With respect to Western Europe, the Kennedy administration underestimated those forces within the Common Market that wanted a European community rather than an Atlantic community, at first regarded De Gaulle as a kind of maverick without group support for his position, and framed the Trade Expansion Act of 1962 in such a way that the most decisive tariff cuts between the United States and the Common Market would depend upon Britain's inclusion in the Market. Nevertheless, the Act as written still allowed for much liberalization of trade, even with Britain outside the Market, and the responsibility for failure to take advantage of this opportunity must be borne by parochial-minded groups and interests inside the Market.

The Kennedy administration's contributions to national defense were notable. It emphasized a balanced and diversified establishment—both strategic and tactical nuclear weapons, conventional arms, and guerrilla forces—so the nation would never have to make the choice between the ultimate weapons and no other adequate defense. It was realistic in its shift from bombers to missiles as the chief nuclear carriers of the future, and in its dismantling of the intermediate missiles bases in Britain, Italy, and Turkey as the Polaris submarines and intercontinental missiles became increasingly operational. Its attempt to find a formula for a NATO multilateral nuclear force was a way of countering De Gaulle's blandishments to the West Germans and of balancing the possibility of a *détente* with Russia with reassurances to Bonn. Its experiments with massive airlifts of ground troops was in part a response to the desires of many of America's NATO allies for less rigidity, less insistence on fixed ground quotas, and more flexibility. However, NATO was plainly in transition, and while the Polaris submarines and intercontinental missiles were making the United States less dependent on European bases, ways were not yet actually implemented to share America's nuclear weapons with European allies on a genuine multilateral basis and satisfy their desires for less centralized direction from the United States.

There was an honest facing up to the terrible responsibilities inherent in the nuclear deterrent. That deterrent was put under tighter control to guard against accident and mistake, and the "hot line" between Washington and Moscow was set up. A much more determined effort was made to get arms-control agreements and a treaty banning nuclear-weapons testing than had ever been made by Kennedy's predecessors. Negotiations with the Soviet Union had been going on for years, but the Americans now so yielded in their former demands for strict international inspection as to put the Russians on the defensive, making world opinion for the first time believe that it was the Russians and not the Americans who were the obstructionists. Kennedy's administration believed that the United States and Russia had an enormous common interest in preventing the spread of nuclear weapons to other countries, that the Sino-Soviet rift gave Khrushchev a new freedom and a new urge to make agreements, and that the increasing accuracy of national detection systems made the possibility of cheating on a test-ban treaty, even one without international inspection, "vanishingly small."

Kennedy's regime also showed its international-mindedness in its firm support of the United Nations. It defended the Secretariat, the executive, from Soviet attacks, and in practice the activities of the Secretariat were widened. The organization was saved from bankruptcy by American financial aid. The operation of the United Nations military force in the Congo, backed by the United States, showed that the American government had no sympathy for "neocolonialism" as practiced by the Katanga secession, and it added another successful precedent for international enforcement of international decisions.

With respect to the underdeveloped nations, the Kennedy policies paralleled the trend of history. Anti-colonialism and self-determination were more valiantly espoused than in the preceding administrations. The Dulles doctrine that neutralism is "immoral" was abandoned, and neutralism was cordially accepted for nations which wanted it. Neutralism was positively encouraged in Laos and in the Congo. Help to South Vietnam was so hedged as to prevent the guerrilla war there from escalating into another Indo-China war, another Korea. Foreign economic aid was increased. The Food-for-Peace program was expanded. The Peace Corps was launched. The Alliance for Progress, an ambitious economic-aid program in Latin America coupled with domestic reforms, an experiment in "controlled revolution," was undertaken.

However, Kennedy, like his predecessors, did little to make the average American understand foreign economic aid—that it is not only an attempt to raise living standards, prevent Communism, and contribute to the world's economic well-being and stability, but is also a substitute for those obsolete ways in which the old colonialism supplied capital to the underdeveloped areas. Until an American president takes to television and in a series of fireside chats explains to Americans in simple terms the real meaning of the foreign-aid program, that program will be in jeopardy.

The Cuban crisis of October, 1962, provoked by the discovery of secret Soviet intermediate missiles in Cuba, was the high point, the turning point, in the Kennedy administration. Could this crisis have been avoided? This will be debated by future historians. True, Khrushchev could not have declined giving Castro economic aid, technical assistance, and some military help, even had he desired to do so, for to have refused this would have been tantamount to surrendering Communist leadership to the Chinese. But why did he go to the length of planting intermediate-missile bases in Cuba? As an appeasement to the Stalinist and Chinese opposition? As a countermeasure to American missile bases in Turkey (which were soon to be dismantled)? As a means of blackmailing Americans into making a compromise on Berlin? To extract a promise from the Americans not to invade Cuba? Whatever the causes, some future historians will have nagging questions: Might this terrible gamble in nuclear brinkmanship have been prevented had Kennedy previously shown more disposition to come to a *détente* with the Soviet Union by a somewhat clearer recognition of the two Germanies and other *de facto* boundaries and arrangements in East and Central Europe; and if so, did this Kennedy reluctance, coming in part out of regard for West German opinion, represent a realistic appraisal of the world situation?

Anyway, when the crisis came, even neutralist opinion seemed to feel that Khrushchev's attempt to compensate for his own intercontinental-missiles lag and the open and avowed American intermediate missiles in Turkey did not justify the sneaky Soviet operation in Cuba. America's quiet, deliberate planning of countermeasures, both military and diplomatic, was masterly. America's prudent use of force, enough but not more than enough to achieve its objective, won world-wide acclaim. Khrushchev and Castro lost face. The Chinese denounced the Soviet backdown, and Chinese-Russian relations worsened. Most important, the peak of the crisis, a spectacular nuclear brinkmanship, cleared the atmosphere like a bolt of lightning. The lunacy of an ultimate nuclear showdown was traumatically revealed. Khrushchev's personal correspondence to Kennedy, reputedly revealing a highly emotional state and a genuine horror of nuclear war, the President had the grace, sportsmanship, and wisdom to keep secret.

Thereafter Khrushchev spoke even more insistently about the need to avoid nuclear war and pursue a policy of peaceful but competitive coexistence. From then on Kennedy gave more public recognition to emerging new international realities, the world's escape from monolithic threats, the trend to pluralism and diversity. In his address at American University in June, 1963, Kennedy spoke as if the Cold War scarcely existed and emphasized the common stake both the United States and the Soviet Union had in world peace and stability. This address, one of the noblest and most realistic state papers of our time, will be remembered long after Kennedy's inaugural address is forgotten.

The new spirit in world affairs expressed itself concretely in the consummation of the limited nuclear test-ban treaty in the summer of 1963, the first real break in the American-Soviet deadlock. After this, Kennedy proposed a joint American-Soviet effort to explore the moon, and he agreed to permit the Soviet Union to purchase American wheat.

By 1963, then, Kennedy had come to much awareness that the postwar world was ending and to a determination to attempt more shifts in American foreign policy in harmony with the emerging fluidity. By this time, too, he had developed close personal relations with a large number of premiers and heads of state the world over. It was felt that after his re-election in 1964 he would be in an unusually strong position to give American foreign policy a new direction, that the test-ban treaty was but a foretaste of more significant measures yet to come, measures which might lead to an American-Soviet *détente,* eventually even to a *rapprochement.* Thus the President's life ended in a tragic sense of incompleteness and unfulfillment.

Every twentieth-century American president with a flair for world politics and in power in time of momentous international decision has been felled by sickness or death before his term was over, before his work was completed. First Wilson. Then Roosevelt. Then Kennedy. For sheer bad luck, this is a record unique among nations.

nine
the missile crisis: soviet objectives appraised

ARNOLD L. HORELICK

*As a senior staff member of the RAND Corporation, the
private "think-tank" involved in research on defense
problems, Arnold L. Horelick has studied extensively
American and Russian military strategies in the nuclear
age. He is the coauthor of* Strategic Power and Soviet
Foreign Policy *(1966), and the coeditor of* La
Guerre Nucleaire *(1965). Born in 1928, Horelick
received his undergraduate education at Rutgers University
and an M.A. from Harvard University; he has been
with the RAND Corporation since 1958. In the
following article from* World Politics, *Horelick analyzes
the background of the Cuban missile crisis. Following
some of the points suggested in the preceding selection
by Ulam, Horelick maintains that the Soviet Union
sought to force American concessions in Europe by
gaining a strategic advantage in Cuba. In arriving at his
conclusions with respect to Soviet motivation,
however, does Horelick adequately refute other possible
Soviet goals, such as the defense of Cuba against
American invasion? Does Adam Ulam's analysis of
Khrushchev's diplomacy suggest Soviet objectives besides
those identified by Horelick? Could Horelick's
definition of Soviet goals perhaps be more explicit?
Accepting Horelick's argument, was the American
response measured and appropriate?*

Source: Arnold L. Horelick, "The Cuban Missile Crisis: An
Analysis of Soviet Calculations and Behavior," *World
Politics* 16 (April 1964): 363–89. Copyright © 1964 by
the RAND Corporation, published by Princeton
University Press. Reprinted by permission of the publisher.

In a television interview not long after the Cuban missile crisis of October 1962, President Kennedy observed that both the United States and the Soviet Union had made serious miscalculations in the Cuban affair. "I don't think we expected that he [Khrushchev] would put the missiles in Cuba," he said, "because it would have seemed such an imprudent action for him to take. . . . He obviously thought he could do it in secret and that the United States would accept it."

As it turned out, of course, deploying strategic missiles in Cuba *was* an imprudent thing for Khrushchev to do, and his expectation that the United States would accept it proved to be mistaken. In the first few weeks after the immediate crisis was resolved by Khrushchev's withdrawal of the Soviet missiles, Soviet affairs specialists turned their attention to the puzzling questions raised by his behavior: (1) Why did Khrushchev deploy strategic weapons in Cuba? (2) What led him to believe he could succeed? (3) Why did he withdraw the weapons so precipitately?

In the months that have elapsed since the first post-crisis flurry of speculation and analysis, a great deal of valuable new information has come to light, particularly in testimony before Congressional committees by high Administration officials. In mid-December 1962, Khrushchev broke the silence he had maintained for some six weeks and presented before the USSR Supreme Soviet the first in a series of detailed explanations of his actions.

Although the new American and Soviet materials for the most part bear only indirectly on the questions posed above, they provide an improved basis for attempting to answer them. One minor participant in the events of October 1962, Fidel Castro, reportedly told a friendly French correspondent that the answers to these questions are "a mystery" which may perhaps be unraveled by historians "in 20 or 30 years." Yet if we are to derive any useful foreign policy and defense lessons from the Cuban missile crisis, we can hardly wait that long. Though these questions cannot now be resolved definitively, we must at least arrive at some provisional answers that can be tested against Soviet behavior in the coming months and years. If we fail to do this, we reduce the momentous U.S.-Soviet Caribbean confrontation of October 1962 to mere episodic proportions.

I.   SOVIET OBJECTIVES

Unfortunately, much of the early post-crisis discussion of Soviet objectives was strongly conditioned by observers' attitudes toward the policy pursued by the U.S. Government in dealing with the crisis and by their appraisals of the probable consequences of its outcome. Among those who criticized the Administration for acting recklessly as well as among those who regarded its policy as too cautious, the argument was encountered that the Soviet Union, directly or indirectly, had achieved much of what it intended.[1] In part,

[1] Professor Leslie Dewart, who argued that the President played into Khrushchev's hands by *over*-reacting, wrote that "yielding was the essence of the [Soviet] scheme." "The conclusion appears reasonable that Russia set up missile bases in Cuba in full knowledge or expectation of the consequences. It is those very consequences [to compel a shift from "rigidity to negotiableness" in U.S. foreign policy] which she can be presumed to have

perhaps, what brought critics of widely divergent political persuasions to
similar conclusions was a shared image, born of Sputnik, of the ten-foot tall
Russians who rarely do anything wrong, and a complementary, equally
erroneous image, fostered by the U-2 and the Bay of Pigs debacles, of
U.S. Administrations that rarely do anything right. But to regard the outcome
of the Cuban missile crisis as coinciding in any substantial way with Soviet
intentions or interests is to mistake skillful salvage of a shipwreck for
brilliant navigation. If the success achieved by the United States in October
1962 proved to be more limited in scope than many believed it would be or
had to be, the outcome hardly constituted a net gain for the Soviet Union.

Some observers have imputed to the Soviet Union precisely those objectives
they believe that Khrushchev achieved: the securing of desired political
concessions from the United States, such as a public pledge by the President
not to invade Cuba; or more generalized political gains, including credit for
having saved the peace. Even if they had been fully achieved, these objectives
would have been blatantly disproportionate to the means expended, and to
the costs and risks incurred by the Soviet Union in the undertaking. The
Chinese and Albanian Communists, and Castro, too, have correctly—from the
Communist point of view—drawn attention to the emptiness of mere verbal
pledges by the enemy. Moreover, the U.S. Government has withheld a formal
pledge, since one of the conditions for it set forth in the Kennedy-Khrushchev
correspondence, on-site verification, has not been satisfied. Khrushchev has
publicly treated the President's conditional pledge as if it were in full force
because he has little else to show for his efforts. While Castro has complained
formally to UN Secretary-General U Thant that "officials of the U.S.
Government declare that they do not consider themselves bound by any
promise," Khrushchev has prudently chosen to ignore these statements.

As to any credit Khrushchev may have gained for saving the peace, it is
doubtful whether his "reasonableness" persuaded many observers of his

sought." ("Russia's Cuban Policy and the Prospects of Peace," *Council for Correspondence
Newsletter,* No. 21 [October 1962], 17, 21.)

Stuart Chase has similarly suggested that "it is not impossible" that the withdrawal of
Soviet strategic weapons from Cuba "was part of a plan, more political than military, to
secure a pledge against invasion." ("Two Worlds," *Bulletin of the Atomic Scientists,*
xix [June 1963], 20.)

Those who criticized the Administration for reacting too cautiously tended to regard
the outcome of the crisis as coinciding less with specific Soviet intentions than with
general Soviet interests. For example, David Lowenthal wrote: "It is what he [the
President] could have done but did *not* do that will most strongly impress our Communist
foes. He forced them to retract the move, and for a brief while aired their malice before
the world. But he did nothing to penalize an action aimed at inflicting an almost mortal
wound on us, and he even made a noninvasion pledge that had never been given before. . . .
We did not even get the *status quo ante."* ("U.S. Cuban Policy: Illusion and Reality,"
National Review, January 29, 1963, 63.)

Along related lines, Robert D. Crane wrote: "The USSR might conclude that the
United States was content with a vague promise of the verified removal of an indefensible
Communist military gain. The Soviets on the other hand, demanded—and apparently
believed they had received—an assurance against an invasion of Cuba by any country
in the Western Hemisphere, which under the circumstances could amount to the creation
of a new doctrine strongly resembling a Monroe-Doctrine-in-reverse." ("The Cuban
Crisis: A Strategic Analysis of American and Soviet Policy," *Orbis,* vi [Winter 1963],
547–48.)

dedication to peace who were not so persuaded before the crisis. It is more likely that his decision to withdraw the weapons served only to restore the confidence in him of those whose faith was shaken by the disclosure—or rather by Khrushchev's belated acknowledgment—that the Soviet Union had deployed strategic missiles and bombers in Cuba. On the other hand, the ranks of those, both in the Communist camp and outside of it, who regard Khrushchev as an "adventurer" or "capitulator" have certainly been augmented. The growth of such beliefs about Khrushchev is not likely to enhance his future political effectiveness.[2]

Finally, to achieve the limited political objectives imputed to them by those who contend that the outcome of the crisis was the one intended by the USSR, the Soviet leaders need not have invested so heavily or risked so much. At least 42 IL-28 bombers and an equal number of strategic missiles were brought into Cuba by Soviet ships; nine missile sites were established, six of them with four launchers each for the MRBM's, and three of them, fixed sites for the IRBM's, each designed to include four launching positions. Yet a token force of a few conspicuously deployed MRBM's would alone doubtless have sufficed to provoke a U.S. demand that the Soviet Union remove them from Cuba.

The magnitude and character of the Soviet strategic weapon deployment in Cuba cast doubt also on a related hypothesis—namely, that the Soviet Union sought merely to compel the United States to withdraw its missiles from Turkey in exchange for the withdrawal of Soviet missiles from Cuba. Since the United States had only one squadron (15 missiles) of Jupiters deployed in Turkey, only a third the number of MRBM's with a 1,100-mile range known to have been shipped to Cuba would have sufficed to make such a trade seem quantitatively plausible. The costly and essentially unsalvageable fixed sites that were being prepared to receive IRBM's with a 2,200-mile range were altogether superfluous to any intended Cuba-Turkey missile-base exchange since the United States had no equivalent missiles in Turkey, or anywhere else for that matter.

Of course, a mutual withdrawal of missiles from Cuba and Turkey was explicitly proposed by Khrushchev in his October 27 letter to President Kennedy. But the mere fact that Khrushchev proposed such an exchange at one point during the crisis, after the United States had demanded the withdrawal of Soviet strategic weapons, no more proves that this was his objective from the start than his subsequent withdrawal of the missiles without such a *quid pro quo* proves that his ultimate objective was simply to get President Kennedy to promise not to invade Cuba. It is true that the withdrawal of U.S. strategic weapons from Turkey, under apparent Soviet duress, would have given Khrushchev a more tangible return for his trouble than a conditional verbal pledge by the United States not to invade Cuba. It is one thing for the United States and an allied host country to decide jointly to substitute for some bases other means of defense, such as Polaris submarines in adjacent

---

[2] In October 1964 (six months after this article was published), Khrushchev was replaced as Soviet Premier.—Ed.

waters; it is quite another for the United States, under Soviet duress, to withdraw from its bases, regardless of the wishes of its allies.

It seems questionable, however, that the Soviets would accept the costs and risks of deploying missiles in Cuba merely in order to remove them in return for the withdrawal of U.S. missiles from Turkey. The phasing out of U.S. missiles deployed overseas, without a Soviet *quid pro quo,* was already known to have been under consideration long before the October 1962 crisis, though the Soviet leaders may not have been certain regarding U.S. intentions. Moreover, because of geographic considerations and the large U.S. advantage in intercontinental nuclear delivery capabilities, a strategic missile base in Cuba was a far more valuable military asset to the Soviet Union than a comparable base in Turkey to the United States. Finally, as pointed out earlier, if the Soviet leaders intended no more than to lay the groundwork for an agreement on the mutual withdrawal of U.S. and Soviet strategic missiles from Turkey and Cuba, they need not have deployed more than a token force of MRBM's and need not have constructed installations for IRBM's at all. It is more likely that the base-exchange proposal was an improvised or perhaps even a prepared fall-back position to cover unfavorable contingencies, but not the Soviet-preferred culmination of the Cuban venture.[3]

Khrushchev's official rationale is that Soviet strategic weapons were deployed in Cuba solely to defend the island against U.S. attack; and that once the threat of such an attack was removed (by the President's conditional undertaking not to launch one), the Soviet weapons, having served their purpose, were withdrawn and peace was preserved. Of course, even on its own terms this rationale is deficient, for Khrushchev also acknowledged, presumably to demonstrate that his decision to withdraw the missiles was not a needless concession, that he took that decisive step only when urgent word reached him that a U.S. attack on Cuba appeared imminent.

Far from deterring the "imperialists," by giving them, in Khrushchev's words, "a more realistic idea of the danger of thermonuclear war," the discovery of Soviet strategic missiles in Cuba provoked a U.S. naval quarantine, a rapid build-up of U.S. Army and Tactical Air Forces in the southeastern part of the country, and a world-wide alert of the Strategic Air Command. Thus, it would seem, the deployment of Soviet strategic weapons in Cuba did not succeed, as Khrushchev said he had anticipated, "in bringing the aggressors to their senses." In his words: "In the morning of October 27 we received information from our Cuban comrades *and from other sources* which directly stated that this [U.S.] attack would be carried out within the next two or three days. We regarded the telegrams received as a signal of

---

[3] If the base-exchange proposal was a *prepared* fall-back position, the Soviet leaders failed to prepare their propagandists for it. On the same day (October 28, 1962) that it front-paged Khrushchev's base-exchange proposal letter to the President, the Soviet Government newspaper, *Izvestiia,* printed on an inside page a commentary which stated: "There are those in the U.S.A. who speculate that in exchange for denying Cuba the ability to repel American aggression, one might 'give up' some American base close to Soviet territory. . . . Such 'proposals,' if you can call them that, merely serve to betray the unclean conscience of the authors." The editor of *Izvestiia* is Alexei Adzhubei, Khrushchev's son-in-law.

utmost alarm, and this alarm was justified. Immediate actions were required in order to prevent an attack against Cuba and preserve peace."

The action, of course, was Khrushchev's proposal to the President to withdraw from Cuba all the weapons "which you regard as offensive" in exchange for cessation of the quarantine and a pledge by the President not to invade Cuba. It must have appeared to Khrushchev, then, that the United States had not only been prepared to attack Cuba *despite* the presence of Soviet weapons, but precisely *because* the weapons had been brought in, since evidently only by agreeing to withdraw them did Khrushchev believe he could secure from the President assurances that the United States would not attack. Presidential statements, made repeatedly in the months preceding the deployment of Soviet missiles in Cuba, that the United States did not intend to invade if offensive weapons were *not* deployed in Cuba, had apparently not been deemed sufficient; only when such an assurance was made conditional on the removal of Soviet strategic weapons from Cuba, with appropriate international verification, did it become acceptable.

The strange logic of Khrushchev's face-saving explanation of Soviet motives and behavior does not in itself disprove his contention that Soviet missiles were deployed in Cuba solely to deter a U.S. attack; it only indicates that if deterrence of a U.S. attack on Cuba was the sole Soviet objective, the plan backfired: the Soviet weapons provoked rather than deterred.

But there are other reasons for doubting Khrushchev's account of Soviet objectives. These have to do with the appropriateness of the weapons selected to be deployed in Cuba for the ostensible purpose of deterring a U.S. attack on that country. Surely a threat to destroy several southeastern U.S. cities, or even Miami alone, *if credible,* would have been adequate to deter such an attack. For this, tactical missiles with a range of several hundred miles would have sufficed. It could have been claimed that such weapons were designed to strike at airfields and marshaling and embarkation points in the Florida area from which a U.S. invasion might be mounted. Perhaps by employing a high lofting technique, the MRBM's that were deployed and the IRBM's that were being prepared could have been used to strike close-in targets, but such long-range missiles are not designed for that purpose. Whatever marginal incremental values for local deterrence (of an attack on Cuba) might have been obtained by deploying missiles with ranges in excess of several hundred miles was more than outweighed by the added provocation they offered.

Had the Soviet missiles remained in Cuba, declarations regarding the control arrangements established for them would have been important indicators of the objectives the Soviet Union sought to pursue. To maximize the effectiveness of Soviet missiles deployed in Cuba as a deterrent against a U.S. attack on Cuba and to reduce the risk that their employment, in the event of such an attack, would bring down U.S. nuclear retaliation against the USSR, it might have been desirable for Khrushchev to have the U.S. Government believe that the Soviet missiles were at Castro's disposal and under his control.

In the United States Castro had gained a reputation for impulsive, irresponsible behavior. Whether authentic or not, the post-crisis remarks attributed to Che Guevara, that the Cubans were prepared, in the event of a U.S. attack, to strike "the very heart of the United States, including New York," conformed to the image of the Cuban leadership that was widely held in the United States. Once an operational missile capability was established in Cuba, such beliefs on the part of Americans might have lent substantial deterrent value to the missiles deployed in Cuba.

On the other hand, to bring Cuba-based missiles to bear in support of Soviet interests in confrontations with the United States (for example, in Berlin), belief that the missiles were at the disposal of the *Soviet* leaders would have been essential. Until such time as the Soviet Union might wish to bring the missiles so to bear, however, the Soviet leaders probably would have preferred to keep the question of control in an ambiguous state. Vague, generalized statements, such as characterize most Soviet strategic threats, might have been employed.

A consideration of probably lesser importance may have been that a premature explicit announcement on control would have obliged Khrushchev to accept certain political liabilities, regardless of whether he claimed that the Soviet Union retained control over the missiles or not. In either case, Khrushchev would have had to acknowledge that the Soviet Union was engaging in a military practice that he had repeatedly denounced: establishing a strategic base on foreign territory, if he claimed control for the Soviet Union; proliferation of nuclear strategic weapons, if he announced that the missiles had been turned over to Cuba.

On October 22, 1962, President Kennedy impaled Khrushchev on one of the horns of this dilemma by unilaterally resolving the ambiguity: ". . . it shall be the policy of this nation to regard any nuclear missile launched from Cuba against any nation in the Western Hemisphere as an attack by the Soviet Union on the United States requiring a full retaliatory response upon the Soviet Union."

Initially, the Soviet Union attempted to evade the issue by refusing to acknowledge that it had emplaced strategic weapons in Cuba, while affirming in its first official statement on the crisis (October 23) that Cuba alone had the right to decide what kinds of weapons were appropriate for the defense of Cuba. But the same statement, without acknowledging that the military equipment provided to Cuba by the USSR included strategic weapons, also reflected Soviet concern that the U.S. Government might feel impelled to strike quickly to prevent operational missiles from falling into Castro's hands. Thus, the following oblique reassurance was offered: "Nuclear weapons, which have been *created by the Soviet people and which are in the hands of the people,* will never be used for the purpose of aggression."

On the same day, privately, Khrushchev made this reassurance explicit during a three-hour conversation in Moscow with Westinghouse Electric Vice-President William E. Knox, through whom he presumably wished to communicate informally with the U.S. Government. According to Knox, Khrushchev acknowledged that Soviet ballistic missiles had been furnished to Cuba, but were completely controlled by Soviet officers. "But the Cubans were very volatile people, Mr. Khrushchev said, and all of the sophisticated hardware furnished for their defense was entirely under the control of Soviet officers; it would be used only in the event that Cuba was attacked, and it would never be fired except on his orders as Commander in Chief of all of the Soviet Union."

Finally, in his October 27 letter to President Kennedy, the first published Khrushchev letter during the crisis, the Soviet Premier informed the President that "the weapons in Cuba that you have mentioned and which you say alarm you are in the hands of Soviet officers." "Therefore," he went on, "any accidental use of them whatsoever to the detriment of the United States is excluded."

It thus seems clear that despite the advantages to be gained from ambiguity regarding control of the missiles in Cuba, Khrushchev felt compelled to reassure the President explicitly that Castro could not order the missiles to be fired and that there was therefore no need for the United States to make an immediate attack before the missiles became operational in order to forestall a possible irrational act by the "volatile" Cubans. Whatever value the Soviet weapons may have been intended to have as a deterrent of a local U.S. attack on Cuba was seriously diminished by this reassurance.

It is questionable, however, whether deterrence of a local U.S. attack on Cuba was ever regarded by the Soviet leaders as more than a subsidiary and derivative effect of a venture intended primarily to serve other ends. Certainly the size and character of the intended deployment indicate that it was meant to achieve some broader purpose.[4] Castro has been quoted by a friendly source, the correspondent for *Le Monde,* Claude Julien, as having said that the Cuban leaders had considered among themselves the possibility of requesting that the USSR furnish Cuba missiles, but had not come to any decision when Moscow proposed to emplace them: "They explained to us that in accepting them we would be reinforcing the socialist camp the world over, and because we had received important aid from the socialist camp we estimated that we could not decline. This is why we accepted them. It was not in order to assure our own defense, but first of all to reinforce socialism on the international scale. Such is the truth even if other explanations are furnished elsewhere."

Although Castro subsequently issued a refutation of an American press agency version of the Julien interview (not of the original *Le Monde* article),[5]

---

[4] For example, while the threat posed by MRBM's to cities, including Washington, D.C., in the southeastern part of the United States would, if credible, have been adequate to deter a U.S. attack on Cuba, most U.S. strategic bomber and missile bases would have been beyond the range of those weapons. These bases could have been covered by IRBM's.
[5] Havana, *Prensa Latina,* March 22, 1963. Specifically, Castro denied only that "I expressed myself in an unfriendly way at any time about Soviet Prime Minister Nikita Khrushchev." Castro's general refutation pointedly referred only to the UPI version of *Le Monde's* article: "I do not believe that Julien, whom we consider a friend of Cuba, can be guilty of untruths like *some* of the statements the UPI attributes to him." (Emphasis supplied.) The March 22 TASS version of Castro's denial *omitted* both of the statements quoted above.
   After this article was written, Castro was questioned by two other journalists regarding the origination of the plan to deploy Soviet missiles in Cuba. According to Herbert L. Matthews (*Return to Cuba,* Stanford University *Hispanic American Report* series [1964], 16), Castro stated flatly on October 23, 1963, that "the idea of installing the nuclear weapons was his, not the Russians'." However, three weeks later, according to Jean

this quotation has the ring of truth. Of course, the deployment of Soviet missiles in Cuba, to the extent that it would have strengthened the Soviet position in its "world-wide" confrontation with the United States, would also have added credibility to Soviet strategic threats, including the threat to defend Cuba against U.S. attack. In fact, the implication of the official Soviet rationale for deploying strategic weapons in Cuba—namely, that the threat posed to the United States by Soviet weapons *based in the USSR* lacked sufficient credibility to deter a U.S. attack on "socialist" Cuba—is one of the troublesome embarrassments with which Khrushchev has had to deal since the Cuban missile crisis.[6]

Before the crisis, Khrushchev's expressions of strategic support for Cuba were framed in notably cautious and equivocal terms: the USSR's capability to defend Cuba with Soviet-based missiles was affirmed, but a commitment to do so was carefully avoided. Cuban leaders, however, consistently interpreted Khrushchev's words as if they represented a firm, though tacit, commitment. For example, according to Guevara, in January 1961 it was already "well known that the Soviet Union and all the socialist states *are ready to go to war* to defend our sovereignty and that *a tacit agreement* has been reached between our peoples."

It may be assumed that the Cuban leaders had pressed Khrushchev for an explicit and unequivocal commitment to defend Cuba with Soviet-based weapons in the event of a U.S. attack. It was presumably to secure such a commitment, which the Soviet Union was evidently reluctant to give, that Castro in effect volunteered Cuba for membership in the "socialist camp" in 1961. As between an explicit and unequivocal Soviet guarantee, on the one hand, and the stationing of Soviet strategic weapons on Cuban soil, on the other, Castro might well have preferred the former under certain circumstances. To the extent that Castro (1) could have had confidence that the Soviet Union would honor such a commitment; or (2) believed that it would be credited to some serious extent in the United States; or (3) believed that a U.S. attack was unlikely in any

---

Daniel's account of his interview with the Cuban Premier, Castro appeared to confirm the account given earlier in the Julien interview: "We thought of a proclamation, an alliance, conventional military aid. . . . They [the Russians] reasoned that if conventional military assistance was the extent of their assistance, the United States might not hesitate to instigate an invasion, in which case Russia would retaliate and this would inevitably touch off a world war. . . . Under these circumstances, how could we Cubans refuse to share the risks taken to save us?" (Jean Daniel, "Unofficial Envoy: An Historic Report from Two Capitals," *New Republic*, December 14, 1963, 18–19.) Matthews writes that he telephoned Castro after Daniel's account was published and was again told: "We were the ones who put forward the idea of the missiles." (*Return to Cuba*, 16.)
[6] Khrushchev handled this question gingerly in defending his Cuban policy against Chinese and Albanian criticism in his speech at the Congress of the SED in Berlin on January 16, 1963: "One may object that, under the influence of the most unrestrained incitement, the U.S. imperialists will not keep their promise and will again turn their arms against Cuba. But the forces which protected Cuba now exist and are *growing in strength every day*. It does not matter where the rockets are located, in Cuba, or elsewhere. They can be used with equal success against any particular aggression." (*Pravda*, January 17, 1963; emphasis supplied.) The implicit question is: If so, why were Soviet missiles deployed in Cuba in the first place? The implicit answer is: Soviet-based strategic power was not *then* great enough to deter a U.S. attack, but it is "growing in strength every day" and soon will be (or will appear to be).

case, he might not have deemed it necessary to request the Soviet Union to establish strategic missile bases in Cuba and might have been wary of the political consequences of such a move at home, throughout Latin America, and in the United States.

For the *Soviet Union* to propose that its strategic weapons be deployed in Cuba, however, may have been another matter. Let us assume that, regardless of the real intentions of the U.S. Government, Castro believed the probability of a U.S. attack was not negligible. He may have agreed to the Soviet proposal not only because of his dependence on the Soviet Union, but also because, from the Cuban point of view, if the Soviet leaders believed their "world-wide" position vis-à-vis the United States was such that it required reinforcement by drastic means, the reliability of Soviet pledges to defend Cuba with Soviet-based weapons—equivocal pledges to begin with—must have seemed seriously compromised.[7]

What was the "world-wide" position of the Soviet Union that needed to be reinforced by the emplacement of strategic weapons in Cuba? Despite boastful Soviet efforts to conceal it, the fact is that throughout the cold war the Soviet Union's capacity to strike the United States with nuclear weapons has been very much smaller than the U.S. capacity to strike the USSR. From the start, the bulk of the USSR's strategic nuclear capability has been effective only out to ranges of about 2,000–2,500 miles. The Soviet Union acquired a very potent nuclear capability against Western Europe, first with medium bombers and then with medium- and intermediate-range ballistic missiles of the type it tried to emplace in Cuba. But the Soviet heavy bomber and ICBM forces—that is, the long-range weapons required to reach the United States—did not attain the strength levels that Western observers anticipated they would reach in the 1960's. Inflated beliefs in the West, actively promoted by misleading and deceptive Soviet claims, that the Soviet Union was rapidly acquiring a large intercontinental strike force tended, until the fall of 1961, to deprive continued and even growing U.S. strategic superiority of much of its *political* value. But, in the second half of 1961, the "missile gap" was found, in Secretary McNamara's words, to be "a myth." Confidence in U.S. strategic superiority was restored in the West; moreover, it became apparent, both from Soviet behavior and from the modification of Soviet strategic claims, that the Soviet leaders knew that the West had been undeceived about the strategic balance.

The deployment of strategic weapons in Cuba may have recommended itself to the Soviet leaders as a "quick fix" measure to achieve a substantial, though far from optimal, improvement in Soviet strike capabilities against the United States. Of course, a large increase in the programmed Soviet-based ICBM force would have provided the Soviet leaders with a military capability far more

---

[7] In the immediate aftermath of the crisis, the pre-crisis positions of the Soviet Union and Cuba on the firmness of Soviet pledges to defend Cuba were sharply reversed. Whereas the Soviet leaders, presumably to placate Castro, offered increasingly strong pledges to defend Cuba, Cuban leaders ignored them and vowed to resist any U.S. attack with their own resources. Later, however, as Soviet-Cuban relations recovered from the estrangement of the fall of 1962, Cuban leaders began to welcome Soviet pledges with great public enthusiasm.

effective (certainly for second-strike purposes) than could be achieved by the emplacement of highly vulnerable MRBM's, IRBM's, and light bombers in Cuba. But such an expansion of the ICBM (and missile-launching nuclear submarine) force could be achieved only gradually and at far greater cost. The Cuban deployment may not have been undertaken as a substitute for such a build-up, but as a stopgap measure, pending its completion.

Certainly the deployment of limited numbers of MRBM's and IRBM's in Cuba would not have solved the Soviet Union's strategic problem. The evident deficiencies of such a force have led some observers to conclude that military considerations were of little importance in the Soviet decision to emplace strategic weapons in Cuba. It is true that the missile sites were soft, very close to the United States, and, after detection, under close and constant surveillance. They would presumably have been highly vulnerable to a U.S. first strike, even with conventional bombs. As a Soviet first-strike force, the Cuba-based force deployed or being readied as of October 1962 was in itself too small to destroy the U.S. strategic nuclear strike force. Even together with the larger long-range strategic force based in the USSR, it seems most unlikely that the force would have been adequate in the fall of 1962; moreover, there would have been a problem, though perhaps not an insurmountable one, of coordinating salvoes from close-in and distant bases so as to avoid a ragged attack. By the same token, however, the installation of Soviet strategic missiles in Cuba would have complicated a U.S. first strike, improved Soviet capabilities to launch a preemptive attack, and hence reduced the credibility of U.S. strategic deterrence of local Soviet aggression, say, in Europe. As to the first-strike potential of Cuba-based Soviet missiles, they could have brought a substantial portion of U.S. nuclear striking power under an attack essentially without warning; moreover, there is no assurance that the build-up would have stopped with the sites already completed or under construction when the Soviets were compelled to abandon the operation.

Whatever their strategic shortcomings, the additional capabilities with which Cuba-based missiles would have provided the Soviet leaders were not insignificant. It is difficult to conceive of any other measure that promised to produce so large an improvement in the Soviet strategic position as quickly or as cheaply. That the Cuban missile deployment would not in itself have provided the Soviet Union with a retaliation-proof first-strike capability against the United States is hardly a reason for dismissing it as of limited strategic importance, as some observers have attempted to do. As the President subsequently said, the Soviet leaders tried materially to change the balance of power. Certainly, the deployment of Soviet missiles in Cuba, in his words, "would have politically changed the balance of power; it would have appeared to [change it] and appearances contribute to reality."

The "world-wide" position of the Soviet Union that needed to be reinforced in the fall of 1962 was not only its strategic position vis-à-vis the United States, but also its position in a range of political issues upon which the strategic imbalance in favor of the United States was having some important bearing. It had become evident, since at least the second half of 1961, that the forward momentum of the Soviet Union in international affairs had largely exhausted itself without yielding the gains which the Soviet leaders had anticipated and the West had feared since the mid-1950's.

These expectations had been fed by mounting evidence of the growing military, scientific, technological, and economic power of the Soviet Union vis-à-vis the West. Some of this evidence was real enough, but much of it, particularly in the realm of strategic power, was illusory. In the framework of the cold war, precisely this realm was central. The effects of other striking achievements, as, for example, in space exploration, were amplified, sometimes out of all proportion to their intrinsic political and military worth, by their presumed bearing on the strategic balance. With the discovery that the "missile gap" had failed to materialize, or had actually materialized in reverse, there was a perceptible change in the world political climate. Western self-confidence was restored and Soviet anxieties must have grown.

Moreover, confident Soviet expectations of a few years earlier in regard to dividends from Soviet military and economic aid to the underdeveloped countries failed to materialize. Western European prosperity had reached a new peak, and despite de Gaulle's intransigence the prospects for growing European economic and political unity must (then, at least) have looked distressingly good to Moscow. At the same time, the unity of the Communist camp was being shattered by the escalating conflict between its two most powerful members. Indeed, the Chinese Communist attack on Khrushchev centered precisely on the unfavorable trend in the cold war which the Chinese attributed to Khrushchev's faulty and overcautious leadership.

Finally, there was the long-smoldering, still unresolved problem of Berlin. After almost four years of threats and retreats, Khrushchev had still not succeeded in compelling the West to accept a Berlin settlement on Soviet terms. Khrushchev may therefore have sought some quick and dramatic means for achieving a breakthrough that would strengthen the USSR's position—militarily, diplomatically, and psychologically—on a whole range of outstanding issues, and particularly on Berlin.[8]

Rarely, if ever, are such fateful ventures as the Soviet strategic deployment in Cuba undertaken to achieve narrow or isolated objectives. Where nuclear weapons are involved, even small risks are acceptable only if important interests can be advanced by assuming them. It is most unlikely that the Soviet leaders drew up a precise blueprint or detailed timetable for exploitation of the improved military-political position they would have attained had the Cuban venture been successful. But they probably anticipated that the emplacement of

---

[8] A link between the Cuban missile deployment and Khrushchev's Berlin strategy was suggested by the Soviet Government's statement of September 11, 1962, in which the USSR acknowledged that it was providing military assistance—though of a strictly defensive type—to Cuba, and warned that a U.S. attack on Cuba might unleash the beginning of a thermonuclear war, but at the same time declared a moratorium on new moves in Berlin until after the U.S. Congressional elections. (*Pravda,* September 11, 1962.) Khrushchev may have hoped to discourage any new U.S. action in regard to Cuba until after the elections (i.e., until after the MRBM's, at least, became operational), by offering, in return, to desist from fomenting a new crisis in Berlin, and then, after establishing a strategic base in Cuba, to use this new levarage to press for a favorable settlement in Berlin.

strategic missiles in Cuba and their acceptance by the United States would contribute in some degree to the solution of a whole range of military-political problems confronting the Soviet Union and would alter the environment of the cold war in such a manner as to promote new opportunities for political gain whose nature could not be precisely foreseen.

II. SOVIET PRE-CRISIS CALCULATIONS

Granted that the stationing of strategic missiles in Cuba promised to be advantageous to the Soviet leaders for a variety of reasons; granted even that the pay-offs seemed so alluring as to justify the assumption of greater risks than they had taken in previous cold war maneuvers, still the question remains: What led the Soviet leaders to believe they could succeed?

With the benefit of hindsight, many Western observers have concluded that Khrushchev's bold move in Cuba was doomed to failure from the start. This in turn has led to the conjecture that Khrushchev never intended to leave the missiles in Cuba, but wished merely to exact political concessions from the United States in return for their withdrawal. This supposition has already been examined and rejected. Others, who also believed the odds against success for the Soviets were very high, concluded that Khrushchev's Cuban gamble explodes one of the articles of faith of Kremlinologists about Bolshevik behavior—namely, the tenet that holds that good Bolsheviks will not engage in adventurism, adventurism being defined as the taking of even small risks of large catastrophes, such as the destruction of the citadel of communism, the Soviet Union. Certainly if it were true that Khrushchev, in undertaking to deploy strategic missiles in Cuba, consciously and deliberately accepted the risk that by this action alone he might bring down a thermonuclear attack upon the Soviet Union, this indeed would have signified a sharp and very dangerous break with past Soviet practice, perhaps the initiation of a new and more ominous phase of the cold war.

But while the Soviet leaders evidently did accept some unusually high military and political risks in embarking on the Cuban venture, the risk of an immediate U.S. thermonuclear response against the Soviet Union was almost certainly not one of them. Moreover, whatever errors they may have made in anticipating the character and intensity of the U.S. response, they were doubtless correct in excluding that one. This established a very crucial upper limit on the risks they did willingly accept.

Given the considerable margin of American strategic superiority which the emplacement of Soviet missiles in Cuba was intended to reduce, on what grounds could the Soviet leaders be confident that the United States would not launch a first strike against the USSR in order to forestall an unfavorable change in the strategic balance? Throughout the cold war, Soviet leaders have demonstrated great confidence in their ability to control the danger of thermonuclear war by means other than the possession of very large intercontinental strategic capabilities. This was true when the strategic balance was far more unfavorable to the Soviet Union than it was in October 1962.

In part this confidence has been based on the powerful indirect deterrent threat of Soviet military power, at first only conventional, and then nuclear, poised to strike Western Europe, the hostage. Later it was reinforced by the threat of even a quantitatively modest intercontinental strike force and of growing U.S. uncertainty regarding the size of that force and the possible upper limits of damage that it could inflict upon the United States. But chiefly the grounds for this confidence have been political. Even when the United States enjoyed decisive strategic superiority, its leaders showed themselves to be strongly disinclined to initiate general war so long as the Soviet Union avoided extreme measures of provocation that could not be dealt with by other means. Increasingly it must have appeared to the Soviet leaders that nothing short of the actual *application* of violence against the United States or an important U.S. ally would risk a U.S. nuclear attack on the Soviet Union. Of course, lesser forms of provocation might create a situation in which the danger of thermonuclear war might be raised to higher levels, but in such cases the Soviet leaders have always allowed themselves ample room for maneuver, and, if necessary, retreat (as in Berlin). They have evidently estimated that sufficient *time* would be available to permit them to extricate themselves from a dangerous situation before it could become uncontrollably dangerous.

The history of the cold war demonstrates that the Soviet leaders have sufficient reason for such an estimate. This estimate is crucial for assessing Soviet risk calculations in Cuba. If one excludes from Soviet pre-crisis calculations serious concern that the United States, even if it detected the missile build-up before completion, would launch a thermonuclear attack against the Soviet Union, then the venture no longer appears to have been a reckless long-shot gamble, but a more familiar calculated and limited risk accepted for sufficiently weighty stakes. This does not mean that as the crisis unfolded the Soviet leaders did not become concerned that a situation might be arising in which a real danger of nuclear war might be created. In fact, the quick withdrawal of their missiles, as we shall see, may be interpreted as a decision to end the crisis quickly before it became necessary to accept even greater losses which could be avoided, if at all, only at the cost of facing serious risk of nuclear war.

Confidence that their action would not directly provoke nuclear war was a prerequisite for embarking on the Cuban missile venture, but it could not be a sufficient condition for success. What then, aside from their belief that the United States would not respond by striking the Soviet Union, were the calculations that led the Soviet leaders to believe their venture could succeed?

Undoubtedly, the Soviet leaders' understanding (or misunderstanding) of U.S. Cuban policy was a major factor in their decision. The ill-fated Bay of Pigs invasion attempt of April 1961, while it may have demonstrated the depths of U.S. hostility toward Castro, may have also suggested to the Soviet leaders that U.S. reluctance to engage its own forces directly in military action against Cuba was so great that even the emplacement of Soviet strategic weapons on the island would be tolerated, or at least resisted by means short of the direct use of U.S. armed forces. At the same time, the fact that the United States had attempted, even though ineffectually, through the use of Cuban exile proxies, to overthrow Castro, both increased Castro's desire for Soviet military assistance and made such assistance seem legitimate to many third countries.

The U.S. Government's apparent acceptance of increasingly open Soviet involvement in Cuban affairs after the Bay of Pigs incident, including particularly the Soviet military involvement, may have strengthened the belief of the Soviet leaders that the United States would engage in armed intervention only in response to the actual use of Cuba-based weapons against some Western Hemisphere country.

The Soviet arms build-up in Cuba was conducted in fairly distinct phases, beginning with the delivery of basic conventional weapons, then working up to more sophisticated weapon systems of a tactical type, and finally to advanced SA-2 surface-to-air missiles, which had been at least partially deployed before strategic missiles were introduced into the island in September 1962. Doubtless the U.S. reaction to the arrival of each new type of weapon was closely observed in Moscow. However, the problem of interpretation must have become increasingly difficult over time, because as the character of the weapons shipped to Cuba grew more complex, their delivery and deployment became increasingly covert; hence, there must have been some uncertainty as to whether the U.S. Government was tacitly accepting the presence of new Soviet weapons or had not yet learned of their arrival. If so, the Soviet leaders evidently resolved these uncertainties in favor of assuming U.S. toleration.

However, if the Soviet leaders had placed a permissive interpretation on generalized statements by U.S. leaders during July and August 1962, regarding "defensive" (acceptable) and "offensive" (unacceptable) Soviet weapons in Cuba, the President on September 4 and again on September 13 explicitly placed surface-to-surface missiles in a category which the U.S. Government considered "offensive," and, hence, unacceptable. Moreover, the President stated specifically on the second occasion that U.S. action would not have to await some overt act, but would occur "if Cuba should possess a capacity to carry out offensive actions against the United States."

The President's first explicit statement on surface-to-surface missiles came several days before the earliest date that the first Soviet missiles and associated equipment, clandestinely transported to Cuba in the holds of large-hatch Soviet ships, are estimated to have reached Cuban ports—around September 8. The second statement, which warned that the mere presence of such weapons, even without any overt act, would require the U.S. Government to act, was made before the earliest estimated date for the initiation of site construction and deployment activity, between September 15 and 20. Thus, the Soviets had two opportunities, shortly before their plan to emplace strategic missiles in Cuba entered its final and decisive phases, to reconsider their decision in the light of evidence of a U.S. commitment to oppose. The President's warnings may have raised anxiety in Moscow, but they clearly did not deter the Soviet leaders. Why?

Assuming that the Soviet leaders regarded the President's statements as a commitment by the U.S. Government to take some kind of action to oppose the emplacement of Soviet strategic weapons in Cuba, they may have believed that, at least initially, the United States would restrict itself to diplomatic means.

They may further have relied on their ability to achieve an operational capability with the missiles quickly enough to ensure the success of the venture. The deployment was carried out with a rapidity that the U.S. intelligence community found "remarkable." Had the Soviets succeeded in achieving their evident objectives of attaining an operational capability clandestinely and then confronting the United States with a *fait accompli,* the outcome *might* have been different. (However, the difference that a *fait accompli* need have made should not be exaggerated.) Speaking of the week-long deliberations that preceded the President's crucial decision in October, Theodore C. Sorensen, special counsel to the President, said that the pressure of time was keenly felt: "For all of us knew that, once the missile sites under construction became operational, and capable of responding to any apparent threat or command with a nuclear volley, the President's options would be drastically changed."

However, the Soviet leaders may not have relied entirely on avoiding detection before completion of the missile deployment, although this was doubtless their preference. Given the difficulties involved in maintaining complete secrecy and the apparent willingness of the Soviets to trade off some possible measures of concealment for greater speed, they could not exclude the possibility that some evidence of the deployment would be at the disposal of the U.S. Government before it could be completed. Allegations, sometimes attributed to Cuban refugees and sometimes even to unnamed members of the intelligence community, that Soviet strategic missiles were present in Cuba had been publicized in the United States even before the first shipment of these weapons is believed to have arrived in Cuba. From the Soviet point of view, the airing of these charges may not have been harmful. Since the Administration was obliged publicly to deny these allegations and to insist repeatedly that the Soviet arms build-up in Cuba posed no threat to U.S. security, the Soviet leaders might have calculated that the President and his advisers, having thus gone on record, would hesitate to charge the Soviet Union with installing offensive weapons in Cuba so long as the evidence placed before them was ambiguous. Moreover, the Soviet leaders may also have believed that the Administration would be reluctant to expose the Soviet Union publicly on the eve of national elections out of concern for unfavorable domestic political repercussions that might be expected if the elections were held with the missiles still in Cuba and no Soviet commitment to withdraw them.

In general, the Soviet leaders probably believed that time worked in their favor and that it was therefore necessary to utilize deception and diplomacy to gain it. They could hardly have expected to be able to maintain their deception indefinitely; indeed, the objectives they pursued required at some point that the new Soviet military capabilities be discovered or revealed. In the event of premature detection, the Soviet leaders may have relied on diplomacy to take over from deception. They probably viewed the likelihood of a strong U.S. reaction as declining over time as numbers of Soviet strategic missiles became operational and the American people and their government grew "accustomed" to the fact of their presence in Cuba.

The Soviet leaders may have come to the conclusion, based on their past experiences with and understanding of the U.S. decision-making process, that the ability of the U.S. Government to assess the situation rapidly and to plan and implement a policy for dealing with it quickly was severely constrained. They may also have counted for time on the likelihood that the U.S. Government would first have to consult with its NATO allies, who could be expected, at the least, to take a less urgent view of the situation than the U.S. Government. They may also have expected that there would be some significant opposition in the Organization of American States to any U.S. proposals for immediate joint action requiring the use of military forces. In short, the Soviet leaders probably estimated that the likelihood of prompt unilateral action by the United States was small. Moreover, they may have reckoned on reducing this probability even more by presenting the United States with a *fait accompli* of such a nature that the prompt unilateral action to reverse it would appear to the U.S. Government to require the initiation of violence.

If these were some of the calculations of the Soviet leaders, events proved them to be wrong on almost every point. This must have come as a great shock to them. The collapse of confidence which evidently caused Khrushchev on October 26 to send off to President Kennedy a private communication in which he reportedly indicated that he was prepared to yield may have been the culminating point of a whole series of disappointed expectations. Because these expectations were not realized, however, does not necessarily mean they were without reasonable bases. Many observers in the West, too, were surprised— though pleasantly—at the speed and efficiency with which the U.S. Government moved, once reliable evidence of the Soviet strategic weapon build-up in Cuba became available.

One other consideration that may have weighed heavily in Soviet planning must be mentioned here—Berlin. If, contrary to probable Soviet expectations, the U.S. Government deemed military action to be an appropriate response, and if the presence of Soviet missiles in Cuba, even supposing them to be operational, proved in itself insufficient to deter such action, the Soviet leaders may still have hoped that the United States would be restrained by fear of possible Soviet retaliation in Berlin. Eighteen months earlier, at the time of the landings in the Bay of Pigs, Khrushchev had in his first letter to President Kennedy obliquely invoked the threat of Soviet retaliation in another part of the world in response to U.S. intervention in Cuba: "We are sincerely interested in a relaxation of international tension, but if others choose to aggravate it, we shall reply in full measure. And in general, it is hardly possible to handle matters in such a way as to settle the situation and put the fire out in one area while kindling a new conflagration in another area."

Whether the Soviet leaders were actually prepared to retaliate in Berlin in October 1962 is another matter ,which we shall later consider. But there was no lack of evidence available to the Soviet leaders to make it appear plausible to them that U.S. policy on Cuba might be influenced critically by U.S. concern over the threat to West Berlin.

For example, in his press conference of August 29, 1962, President Kennedy directly linked U.S. policy on Cuba with U.S. obligations in West Berlin: "The U.S. has obligations all around the world, including West Berlin . . . , and therefore I think that in considering what appropriate action we should take we have to consider the totality of our obligations and also the responsibilities we bear in so many different parts of the world."

That U.S. planners were concerned during the Cuban crisis about possible Soviet counteraction in Berlin has been widely reported. In his October 22 speech, the President made a special point of warning the Soviet leaders against such a course of action: "This latest Soviet threat or any other threat which is made either independently or in response to our actions this week must and will be met with determination. Any hostile move anywhere in the world against the safety and freedom of peoples to whom we are committed, including in particular the brave people of West Berlin, will be met by whatever action is needed."

If the Soviet leaders had hoped that such concerns would inhibit a strong U.S. reaction to their deployment of strategic weapons in Cuba, events, of course, proved them to be mistaken. But, again in this regard, their expectations were not entirely without foundation.

III.   SOVIET CRISIS CALCULATIONS

We have now arrived at the third of the three questions posed at the beginning of this paper: Why did Khrushchev change course so precipitately and withdraw his strategic missiles and bombers from Cuba? Implicitly, some reasons have been adduced in the preceding discussion of probable Soviet pre-crisis miscalculations. It remains to make these points explicit and to amplify them.

(1) The Soviet leaders had evidently hoped to present the United States with a *fait accompli* in Cuba (like the hastily erected Berlin wall in August 1961). As it turned out, however, the Soviet deployment was not yet completed when the President instituted the quarantine and demanded the withdrawal of Soviet strategic weapons. The U.S. Government had more freedom of choice and action than the Soviet leaders probably foresaw.

(2) By effectively preserving secrecy regarding the response it had chosen to make, the U.S. Government, on October 22, was able to present the Soviet Union with what was, in some sense, an American *fait accompli*: the quarantine.

(3) The character of the U.S. response, as set forth by the President on October 22, apparently confounded the Soviet leaders. By imposing a quarantine on strategic arms shipments to Cuba as the first in a series of measures designed not only to prevent a further build-up, but to secure the removal of weapons already on the island—the other measures remained deliberately unspecified— the United States in some sense shifted on to the Soviet side the immediate burden of decision regarding the precipitation of violence. As an initial response the quarantine was considerably less than a direct application of violence, but considerably more than a mere protest or verbal threat. The U.S. Navy placed itself physically between Cuba and Soviet ships bound for Cuban ports. Technically, it might still have been necessary for the United States to fire the first shot had Khrushchev chosen to defy the quarantine, though other means of preventing Soviet penetration might have been employed. But once the quarantine was effectively established—which was done with great speed—it

was Khrushchev who had to make the next key decision: whether or not to risk releasing the trip-wire.

In dealing with the quarantine itself, the Soviet leaders essentially had three choices, all of them unpleasant, and one of them quite dangerous: (1) They could submit to the quarantine by permitting their vessels to be stopped, searched, and, if they carried contraband, to be seized; or (2) they could avoid a showdown by keeping their ships out of the quarantine area—which, with the exception of an oil tanker clearly identifiable as such, is what they actually did; or (3) they could precipitate the use of violence by attempting to violate the quarantine, perhaps with the aid of submarines. Soviet prospects for success in such an undertaking were very poor; and the outlook could not have appeared any brighter to them at any of the successively higher local levels of violence that could be contemplated.

(4) U.S. success in securing prompt and unanimous support for the quarantine in the OAS and the active participation of naval elements from some Latin American countries in the operation must have made the Soviet leaders pessimistic about the chances of bringing diplomatic pressure effectively to bear on the United States to lift the quarantine. This may have caused the Soviet leaders to regard a "waiting strategy" as less promising diplomatically than they had anticipated, while the U.S. military preparations also made such a strategy appear increasingly risky.

(5) The President's decision to confront the Soviet Union directly and to ignore Castro also compelled the Soviet leaders to determine their course of action quickly. It removed the ground from under any Soviet effort to involve the United States in negotiations with the Cuban Government, as the Soviet leaders subsequently attempted unsuccessfully to do in connection with the IL-28 bombers. Diplomatically and morally, the U.S. decision to confront the Soviet Union directly made it possible to separate the specific issue of the menacing Soviet weapon deployment in Cuba from the broad and controversial issue of U.S.-Cuban relations.

(6) Finally, there was the speed and evident resolution with which the U.S. Government acted in the Cuban missile crisis. This refers not only to the prompt and successful implementation of the quarantine, the rapid securing of OAS cooperation and NATO support, but above all to the speed and impressiveness of the U.S. conventional military build-up in the southeastern states and of the alert measures taken by U.S. strategic forces around the world. There is no doubt that these preparations were carefully noted by Moscow, and we can probably take at face value Khrushchev's statement of December 12, 1962, that he took his decision to withdraw Soviet missiles from Cuba after receiving urgent word that a U.S. attack was imminent. These preparations must have persuaded him that he had to act quickly in order to limit his losses. Evidently Khrushchev was unwilling to gamble further on the possibility that the U.S. Government would ultimately stop short of direct military action, for losing such a gamble would have meant accepting far greater local losses, and perhaps even risking general war.[9]

[9] In regard to the role played by the danger of general war in Khrushchev's decision to

Whether it was mainly conventional U.S. military superiority in the Caribbean area or overall U.S. strategic nuclear superiority that won the day—a hotly debated question in the aftermath of the crisis—does not strike this writer as a useful way to pose the problem. The United States possessed superiority of both types and brought both to bear in the crisis: the presence of one reinforced the effectiveness of the other. The *immediate* military threat confronting the Soviet leaders was, of course, that posed locally to Soviet forces in Cuba and to the Castro regime. But this threat was amplified by U.S. strategic superiority, which made credible the announced determination of the U.S. Government to employ force locally if other measures, such as the quarantine, proved inadequate, and to retaliate against the Soviet Union if Cuba-based weapons were launched against targets anywhere in the Western Hemisphere. Extraordinary alert measures taken by the Strategic Air Command, including such conspicuous ones as the dispersal of B-47's to auxiliary civilian airfields, underscored this determination. Manifest U.S. strategic superiority rendered Soviet strategic deterrence of a local U.S. attack on Cuba inoperable.

It may be true that even a strategic balance less favorable to the United States—say, one of acknowledged parity—would have been sufficient to support the policy implemented by the U.S. Government in October 1962; that is, the Soviet leaders would still have been unable to deter a U.S. attack on Cuba by credibly threatening strategic retaliation against the United States. But U.S. strategic superiority also made it too risky for the Soviet Union to play or, under the circumstances, even threaten to play the Berlin trump card. While some Western observers feared that the Soviet Union might attempt to dissuade the United States from calling the Soviet hand in Cuba by threatening to retaliate in Berlin, the Soviet leaders apparently feared that a threatening Soviet move in that city, *particularly* in the midst of a crisis in the Caribbean, would be dangerously provocative. Emphasizing that the Cuban crisis "had brought the world one step, perhaps only half a step, from an abyss," Foreign Minister Gromyko told the Supreme Soviet in December 1962: "This [Cuban] crisis . . . made many people think how the whole matter might have developed if yet another crisis in Central Europe had been added to the critical events around Cuba." Indeed, Soviet quiescence in Berlin during and immediately after the Cuban missile crisis demonstrates the severe limitations of even overwhelming local military superiority in the hands of a strategically inferior power when the issue at stake is of central, not peripheral, importance to the opponent.

---

withdraw Soviet strategic weapons from Cuba, Secretary McNamara testified before a Subcommittee of the House Committee on Appropriations in February 1963: ". . . we had a force of several hundred thousand men ready to invade Cuba . . . had we invaded Cuba, we would have been confronted with the Soviets . . . had we been confronted with the Soviets we would have killed thousands of them . . . had we killed thousands of them the Soviets would probably have had to respond . . . they might have had nuclear delivery weapons there [that] might have been operational and they might have been launched . . . in any event, Khrushchev knew without any question whatever that he faced the full military power of the United States, including its nuclear weapons . . . we faced that night the possibility of launching nuclear weapons and Khrushchev knew it,

   The role played by Berlin in the Cuban crisis during the fall of 1962
dramatizes the curious role that threats, expectations, fears, and hopes regarding
that city have played in the cold war since Khrushchev in November 1958
opened the long second round of the East-West struggle over the divided city.
Much of Soviet foreign policy behavior since that time has been interpreted as
maneuvering to secure a stronger position from which to impose on the West
a Soviet-preferred solution of the Berlin "problem." Many regarded the
Cuban missile deployment as designed chiefly to improve the Soviet
bargaining position in the renewed crisis that was expected to be raised by
the Russians after the U.S. elections in 1962. Since the Soviets appeared to be
so intent on securing better leverage in Berlin, it would seem that they regarded
it as too risky to proceed there without such leverage. Yet many who believed
that Berlin was the real objective of the Soviet missile deployment also
believed there was great danger that the Soviet leaders would retaliate in
Berlin for any local defeat inflicted upon them in Cuba by the United States.
The logic is strange: U.S. strategic superiority and the Western allies'
determination to preserve their rights in West Berlin made it too risky for
the Soviets to employ their local military superiority in order to impose a
settlement; yet the West must proceed with great caution elsewhere lest it
provide the Soviet Union with a pretext for imposing its will in Berlin, or
compel the Soviet leaders to do so, even against their better judgment, in
order to "save face" for a defeat in some other part of the world.[10]
   However, the Soviet leaders have never needed pretexts for plucking ripe
fruits from the vine. The foreseeable consequences of a Western defeat in
Berlin provide more than enough incentive for the Soviet leaders to administer
it if they think they can do so safely. Khrushchev's need to "save face" has,
in this writer's opinion, been grossly exaggerated; in any case, the Cuban
missile crisis was not the first occasion on which Khrushchev seemed to be
in need of "face-saving." The four preceding years of bluster and retreat in
Berlin had certainly been "humiliating" enough.
   Hopefully, one lesson that both sides have learned from the Cuban
experience is that, so long as the West maintains a favorable strategic balance,
the Soviet Union cannot use West Berlin as a hostage to cover Soviet offensive
moves and probes in other parts of the world against strong Western
countermeasures. "Hostage Western Berlin" should not be confused with
"Hostage Western Europe." The Soviet threat to strike Western Europe in

---

and that is the reason, and the only reason, why he withdrew those weapons."
(*Hearings*, 31.)
[10] Walter Lippmann continued to argue after the crisis that "it would have been an
incalculable risk to invade and occupy Cuba at the risk of retaliatory military action against
Berlin, action which could have escalated into nuclear war." Yet the Soviet Union evidently
yielded because its leaders found it highly credible that the United States would assume
this "incalculable risk." According to Lippmann, "the United States prevailed in Cuba
because, after nuclear power had been neutralized, it had powerful conventional weapons."
("Cuba and the Nuclear Risk," *The Atlantic*, February 1963, 56, 58.) But if U.S. nuclear
power served no function other than to neutralize that of the Soviet Union, it is difficult
to understand why preponderant Soviet conventional military power has not enabled the
USSR to prevail in Berlin.

the event of a U.S. attack on the Soviet Union is highly credible because the ultimate catastrophe to the USSR would have already occurred when the threat would have to be executed; but to retaliate in West Berlin for some lesser Western "provocation" might cause that very catastrophe to be brought down upon the Soviet Union when it could otherwise be avoided.

part three
coexistence and détente

ten
what's left of
the cold war?

BRIAN THOMAS

*In "What's Left of the Cold War?" British scholar
Brian Thomas analyzes the significance and
ramifications of the decline of the Cold War. Louis
Halle, in* The Cold War as History, *concluded that the
Cuban missile crisis marked the end of the classic
Cold War; Thomas considers this conclusion in the light
of subsequent developments, particularly the
Czechoslovakian crisis of 1968. According to Thomas,
the crisis in Czechoslovakia, like that in Cuba six
years earlier, illustrated the tacit Russian and American
acceptance of spheres of influence based on a balance
of power. Thomas, a senior lecturer in international
relations at the North-Western Polytechnic, London,
took his degree in international relations at the
London School of Economics and later served with the
British Ministry of Defence. He entered politics
briefly, entering two Parliamentary elections as a Labour
party candidate. In addition to the following article,
Thomas has written on the origins of the Cold War
in the* Journal of Contemporary History *and is the
author of* The Fifty Years War: Russia and the
West, 1918–1968. *Do the developments described by
Thomas provide a firm basis for coexistence? Is his
position that ideology has become irrelevant in influencing
Russian-American relations consistent with the
analyses offered in preceding articles?*

Five years, almost to the day, separated the signing of the
test ban treaty from the Soviet invasion of Czechoslovakia.
It was an interval when the question "What's left of the

Source: Brian Thomas, "What's Left of the Cold War?" *The
Political Quarterly* 40 (April–June 1969): 173–86.
Reprinted by permission of the author and the publisher.

Cold War?" was increasingly asked, and when the answer usually given was "Not very much." By 1968 a considerable number had come, as with Louis Halle in his *The Cold War as History* (1967), to view the Cold War as a finite phenomenon with a date at both ends, and the years most commonly chosen were 1947 and 1962.

There still remained much, of course, on which the experts disagreed. There was the difficulty of definition: the Cold War was variously represented as a power struggle, as a conflict of ideologies, as an economic challenge, and as a mixture of the three. There was the Cold War's date of birth: the suggestions offered ranged throughout the thirty months from Truman's accession to Zhdanov's "two camps" speech at the foundation of the Cominform. Finally, there was the question of blame. This was indeed insoluble, largely because of the reluctance of historians who accused the East to subject Western moves to equal scrutiny, and of those who accused the West to distinguish between an analysis of the Cold War and a study of American foreign policy. The one point of substantial agreement centered on the second Cuban crisis. With the Khrushchev-Kennedy confrontation, it was felt, the Cold War in its traditional form had come at last to an end.

THE REAL RESULTS OF CONFRONTATION

There are reasonable grounds for this view, and it has not become less valid since the invasion of Czechoslovakia. Despite all the hopes raised when Stalin's death coincided both with nuclear parity and the ending of the Korean War, the "Geneva summer" failed to last. In the three years immediately before the test ban treaty was signed there were no fewer than four major crises. One was the affair of the U2; two were over Cuba; and the other—the longest and in some respects the most serious—occurred over Berlin. For many they recalled the three years that ended with Korea, and this no doubt contributed to that feeling of acute pessimism which dominated contemporary comment even before the final crisis erupted.

Consequently, the abrupt change of atmosphere which occurred soon after 1962 reminded some of 1953–55; but it soon became plain that the differences were enormously greater than the similarities. Of these the most remarkable was the changed attitude of both Great Powers towards events in what could loosely be called each other's sphere of influence. Throughout 1963 and 1964 the steadily increasing American commitment in Vietnam, although formally objectionable, aroused nothing like the Soviet hostility which met the United States' attempt to dislodge Castro in 1961. This was strange, considering that the threat to the Americans from Cuba had been not only very close at hand; it had posed a direct challenge to that same Monroe Doctrine which Khrushchev himself had praised as originally "positive," "anti-colonialist," and even "democratic." The same could hardly be said of the threat from Vietnam, where the Americans were obliged to rely much more heavily on the "domino" theory to justify their presence. Nonetheless, as time went on it became clear that opposition to America's role in that part of the world was coming much more from unofficial feeling in the West than from any public censure in the East. Any idea that the difference arose from a particular Soviet interest in the Caribbean was soon disposed of; for America's role in the Dominican *coup* of April 1965 drew an equally indifferent response.

It has now begun to look as if a similar change of front has taken place in Washington. The unexpected mildness of the United States' reaction to the Soviet invasion of Czechoslovakia drove some observers, after commenting on the tougher line being taken by the British, to compare it with America's former bluntness over Hungary. They could have gone further. In 1956 Hungary, like Cuba, was close to the Great Power concerned, had long been regarded as inside its sphere of influence, and was protected, if not by a Monroe Doctrine, then by an agreement of a not dissimilar kind signed by Churchill and Stalin in 1944. Czechoslovakia, on the other hand, resembled Vietnam; it was much more on the fringe of a "protected" area, had never as a "liberated state" been officially allotted to one side or the other, and seemed to be less of a really vital interest.

But the most striking change in America's attitude towards successive Soviet moves can be seen not over those which affected Czechoslovakia and Hungary, but over those which affected Czechoslovakia itself. One need only compare the restraint shown over a clear case of aggression in 1968 with the very different reaction to the internal *coup* of 1948. The latter, it will be recalled, led President Truman on March 17 of that year to recommend the resumption of universal military training, on the grounds that the Soviet Union had a clear design to "subjugate the free communities of Europe." No such conclusion seems to have been drawn by President Johnson, despite the fact that Soviet responsibility for the Czech *coup* had to be assumed, whereas there was no doubt at all about who was responsible for the invasion. One may well wonder what has happened since 1962 to cause this change of outlook.

THE ACCEPTANCE OF DEFEAT

Part of the answer lies in the increasing preoccupation of both Powers with their own internal problems, and with those of their own client states rather than each other's. In addition, there seems to be a belated recognition that with the creation of the last group of African states the balance of power in the world is beginning to alter; and that for the first time since 1944 more things are happening to Washington and Moscow than they themselves are causing to happen. Adding weight to this must be the rise of China, perfectly prepared since 1962 to add an open challenge to the Soviet Union to its existing cold war with the United States. From the point of view of Russia's preoccupations, it is worth noting that China's successful nuclear tests of October 1964 preceded both the American action against the Dominican Republic and the bombing of North Vietnam. But, this apart, the suspicion is at least current that in the not too distant future both Washington and Moscow will find themselves in the position of London and Berlin after 1917: centres of continental power destined in course of time to be replaced by others. All this is probable. But what is far more likely is that since 1962 both sides have been considering the political effects of confrontation after fifteen years of preparation. For the most significant result of the confrontation was that neither side gained its objective.

The United States is now obliged as a result of a qualified guarantee to coexist with the Castro regime in Cuba, in permanent breach of the Monroe Doctrine. The importance of this is sometimes overlooked. It is occasionally argued that what the United States objected to was not the existence of an independent communist state inside the American hemisphere, but Castro's subversive role in Central and South America as an agent of the Soviet Union. If this were so then Castro's offer in the summer of 1964 to suspend aid to other American revolutionaries in return for recognition would hardly have been so brusquely rejected, or his many differences with the Soviet Union overlooked. But it was Adlai Stevenson's statement to the United Nations, made shortly before the crisis broke, which put the matter beyond reasonable doubt:

The President of Cuba professes that Cuba has always been willing to hold discussions with the United States to improve relations and to reduce tensions. But what he really wishes to do is to place the seal of approval on the existence of a Communist regime in the Western hemisphere. The maintenance of Communism in the Americas is not negotiable.

This is a point of much more than historical interest; for one has only to change five or six proper nouns in Mr. Stevenson's statement to obtain a precise, almost word perfect copy of the argument *Pravda* was to use six years later to justify the invasion of Czechoslovakia.

The use of this argument by the Russians in August 1968—reinforced with a military invasion—gave some indication of her earlier losses. These were not limited to the withdrawal of the Cuba missiles. She failed also to secure the withdrawal of American rockets from Turkey, in spite of Khrushchev's insistence. Such a negative result at the height of the Cold War would soon have led to retaliatory measures. The end of the Berlin blockade was a powerful spur to NATO; the stalemate in Korea to ANZUS and to SEATO. That the Cuban confrontation led to a *détente* clearly suggests a change of phase; and the explanation, I submit, is military.

THE RUSSIAN THREAT DEVALUED

Throughout the fifteen years before 1962 the West clearly felt the need, for political reasons, to exaggerate in public Russia's military strength. As a rule the figures quoted were correct, but they were usually relayed out of context. The 1948 figure of 2,874,000 for Soviet military manpower, for example, placed beside the American figure of 1,500,000, was the one most frequently used to demonstrate the need for NATO; and in the course of time the figure, along with others, was duly confirmed in a speech of Khrushchev to the Supreme Soviet (January 14, 1960). Compensating factors, however, were almost all omitted. It was rarely suggested, for instance, that the figure quoted for Soviet strength in 1948 was only fractionally larger than the one for 1939, about half of that for 1941, or a quarter of the figure for 1945 (2,300,000, 4,207,000 and 11,365,000 respectively). Neither were any of them set against the contemporary American superiority in atomic weapons, the number and situation of American military bases, or related to the land frontiers the Russians were required to defend. Had they been so, no useful conclusions about aggressiveness could seriously have been drawn, or much doubt felt about the consistent superiority of the West over the whole period.

With the ending of the Cuban crisis, this habit was immediately abandoned. Almost at once published estimates suggested a Western superiority that was certainly comfortable and in some respects overwhelming. For long-range missiles the proportions were revealed as 450–500 for the West and 75 for Russia. Conventional strengths were equally reassuring: NATO, 5,818,500 and the Warsaw Pact countries, 4,354,000; while a figure for the United States alone was given as 2,700,000 and for the U.S.S.R. 2,300,000. Nor, it seemed, need the West feel any qualms over their once vulnerable zone in Central Europe, for there the proportions were: for NATO, 975,000, compared with only 665,000 for the countries of the Warsaw Pact.

As no claim was made—or could have been—that these figures were in any way the result of recent changes, their immediate implications were considerable; and one felt, a week after the test ban treaty was signed, that the Defence Correspondent of *The Times* (August 12, 1963) had disposed of a whole era in three sentences when he wrote:

> *The latest American appraisals of the Soviet military threat to Europe suggest that previous intelligence assessments have consistently overestimated the strength of the Soviet armed forces. Defence planners in Washington and a growing number of military observers in Europe now believe that the apparently large preponderance of Soviet conventional strength upon which much of Western policy and strategy has been based is as illusory as the notorious missile gap which bedevilled military planning in 1960 and 1961. . . . American experts on Soviet foreign policy underline these latest assessments with their own view that Soviet aims in Europe tend towards containment rather than expansion, and that they are in fact preoccupied more with the dangers of an attack from the West than with any aggressive intent of their own.*

At about the same time it was made equally clear that this superiority did not give the West any more freedom of action, or even—as the Czechs were soon to discover—the opportunity to do again what Kennedy had done over Cuba. The imminent Soviet possession of a 100 megaton bomb, even before Khrushchev confirmed it at the Sixth Congress of the German Socialist Unity Party on January 16, 1963, was felt by many Washington observers to mean that never again would any of the Powers risk a repetition of the events of July–October 1962.

A GENUINE BALANCE OF POWER

This reappraisal of the military facts of life marked the end of the Cold War in its traditional form. The long-feared nuclear showdown had in fact taken place, and without either side achieving the breakthrough it had sought since 1947. America's reaction to the invasion of Czechoslovakia can now be understood; and it is a misreading of the position to suggest, as did the Washington Correspondent of *The Times* a month before, that the United States would take no counter-action because "the so-called liberation policy died with the Hungarian intervention of 1956" (July 20, 1968). The question of adopting a liberation policy never arose, and would have been irrelevant if it had. The only positive policy available in 1968 was the traditional one employed over Cuba, that of "negotiation from strength"; and it was deliberately declined.

The effect of this reappraisal on East-West relations is somewhat paradoxical. There seems now to be a genuine balance of power in which both sides are deterred from attacking either each other or each other's obvious satellites. But as neither can impose its will, limited action elsewhere is likely to go unchallenged. Countries inside a Power's sphere of influence which—like Cuba or Hungary—were the subject of bitter argument before 1962 will tend now to be immune from the attentions of the other Power, but not of course from their own; and this immunity will persist whether those attentions take the form of a desire to attack, or—as with the United States and Czechoslovakia—a possible wish to defend. It follows that the big Powers have achieved some security. They are compelled to observe an indefinite and not particularly dangerous armistice. But for many smaller states the position is commensurately worse.

If, then, the spectres of Soviet superiority and American brinkmanship have both been safely laid, and all we have is the normal rivalry of two Great Powers who can be trusted not to take things too far, what remains of the Cold War?

Here definition is important. If by the Cold War we mean simply the breakdown of the accidental alliance of Russia and the West, the alliance caused by the coincidence of *Barbarossa* with Pearl Harbour, the answer is that the breakdown is now complete and that since 1962 "normal," *i.e.,* pre-1941, relations have been resumed. If by the Cold War we mean the West's reaction to Soviet military policies of the post-war years the answer is that this is finished too. American—and other—conclusions that Soviet policy is essentially defensive can be accepted, provided all attempts to preserve Soviet influence in whatever states were subject to it before October 1962 can be regarded as defensive acts. Such states include Cuba, Rumania and Czechoslovakia. They exclude China, Albania and Yugoslavia. Thus the safety of, say, Rumania is by no means guaranteed. There the Russians might well feel, as they felt in Czechoslovakia and as the Americans clearly feel in Vietnam, that the loss of influence in a particular state, however insignificant, would spark off a chain reaction in physically adjacent countries which could lead to a serious weakening of total power. The "domino" theory, on which

the United States relies in Vietnam, is still the most satisfactory explanation
of the invasion of Czechoslovakia.

It so happens that since 1962 this "defensive" view of Soviet power has
been extended backwards in time; and the whole Western post-war policy of
containment now stands condemned by one of its principal authors on the
grounds that it drew "a line arbitrarily across Europe against an attack no one
was planning." Mr. Kennan's corollary, that the same policy—by permitting
"Communist domination to extend farther west than might otherwise have
been the case"—provoked the very aggression it was trying to prevent, still
awaits detailed historical investigation. But one can hardly help reflecting
how close Mr. Kennan has now come to the position occupied by his opponents
of twenty years ago, Senator Taft and Mr. Henry Wallace.

What then is—or was—the threat? Mr. Kennan has an answer, and it
supplies us with a definition of the Cold War that fits the present facts. The
threat, he says, came not from Soviet aggression but from the internal activities
of communist-trained and communist-inspired minorities, to which NATO and
SEATO—but not, I would add, the Truman Doctrine—were irrelevant.

THE COLD WAR REDEFINED

If we think of the Cold War in the sense implied, it appears as the active
preoccupation of both East and West with the spread of communism, which
may or may not coincide with Soviet military aggression. In Czechoslovakia it
did coincide; in Vietnam it does not. This is a definition which fits more
precisely the developments of recent years, just as it does those which obtained
before 1947. Applying it, it seems at once as though the Cold War is by
no means over; but this does not follow. The end of this kind of Cold War
does not depend upon the disappearance of communism inside particular
countries. All that is necessary is for both Powers to agree on how to deal with
it; and in my view that agreement has been reached.

The fact that one Power is termed "capitalist" and the other "communist"
is quite irrelevant in this situation. Neither does it follow that because both are
engaged in fighting communists and anti-communists in different parts of
the world they are bound to fight each other, any more than did Churchill and
Stalin when they made their spheres-of-influence agreement in 1944. On that
occasion Churchill was militarily engaged in Greece and Stalin in Rumania;
and shortly afterwards both turned their attention to communism in those two
countries, Stalin to promote it and Churchill to suppress it. But there was
no disagreement between them. As Churchill himself put it:

> . . . in spite of the fact that all this was most disagreeable to him and
> those around him . . . Stalin . . . adhered strictly and faithfully to
> our agreement of October, and during all the long weeks of fighting
> the Communists in the streets of Athens not one word of reproach
> came from Pravda or Izvestia. . . . If I pressed [Stalin] too much he
> might say, "I did not interfere with your action in Greece; why do

you not give me the same latitude in Rumania?" . . . I was sure it
would be a mistake to embark on such an argument.

Clearly, the Powers did disagree at some stage, and I am suggesting that
that was what the Cold War was about. To be precise, it arose not over what
the Powers did about communism but where they chose to do it. At one
stage—the Cold War proper, if you will—both East and West were actively
concerned over the spread of communism without defining boundaries. The
Russians were concerned to spread it and the West to stop it being spread.
They still are, of course; but the difference is that they now agree on the
boundaries, and with this agreement the Cold War has come to an end.

THE INTRUSION OF IDEOLOGY

What evidence is there for this? I have argued elsewhere that the Soviet
interest in promoting the spread of communism *per se* ceased with the onset
of the depression in the early 1930s, to be replaced by an almost exclusive
concern with the safety of the Soviet state. (Before that, its leaders felt, the
two could not be separated.) After the Second World War, however,
concerned to establish a position of strength in the east of Europe, Stalin once
again identified the spread of communism with the survival of Soviet power,
particularly after 1946. But outside Eastern Europe—in Greece, Yugoslavia,
France, Italy and China—he continued to treat communists with a contempt
that could hardly have been equalled by any of their national opponents; and,
as we have seen in recent months, his successors have done the same.

In much the same way the West, conditioned by their struggle with Nazi
Germany and her allies, which they saw—rightly or not—in ideological terms,
tended to regard the spreading of the Western parliamentary system and its
associated values as a powerful antidote to the outbreak of a third world war.
The Atlantic Charter, the "Declaration on Liberated Europe," and the constant
references to democracy and free elections in the various wartime agreements
furnish ample evidence of this. At Baylor University a week before he
pronounced the Truman Doctrine, President Truman even felt compelled
to add a rider in economic terms, recommending to all the world a pattern of
trade based on free enterprise and the commercial structure of the West.
Looked at in this light, the much criticised "liberation" and "roll-back"
policies of Mr. Dulles, however inadvisable in other ways, were wholly in
keeping with this line of thought. But, as with Russia, the tendency to identify
security with the extension of a particular political system did not last long,
and was inhibited by the growth of the police state in areas well outside the
communist camp.

The present position is that while the West is preoccupied with stopping the
spread of communism—loosely defined to include the Vietcong—outside the
Soviet sphere, the Russians are preoccupied with preserving it inside. In
the case of Czechoslovakia, this is done on the basis of Stalin's principle that
just as the most satisfactory way to include Central Europe inside Russia's
defensive sphere was to instal communism, so the easiest way to lose it is to

allow communism to be weakened out of all recognition. In this context it is as irrelevant whether Dubcek is a genuine "anticommunist" as it is whether the Vietcong are "communists." It is the two Powers who supply the definitions.

In this kind of contest spheres of influence—in which liberals can be safely suppressed and communists successfully fought without danger of retaliation from the other Power—become doubly important. Defining them may prove a source of friction. But provided each Power acknowledges in practice the right of the other to act as it wishes inside a certain zone, a Cold War of this kind is quite unnecessary. But has there been such an acknowledgment? I suggest there has, and that it has been recently revived.

YALTA, MONROE OR TRUMAN?

Looked at in terms of a quest for spheres of influence, East-West relations since Russia entered the war fall into four well-defined parts. The first, beginning with Eden's visit to Moscow in December 1941 and ending in 1944, was concerned entirely with the problem of Russia's post-war frontiers. Stalin insisted on those of 1941, Eden on those of 1938. No agreement was reached; in Eden's words, "with the best will in the world, it was impossible to work with these people." The second was the interval when spheres of influence far in excess of the territory Stalin asked of Eden were drawn up and respected. This phase commenced with the Churchill-Stalin agreement of October 9, 1944, and continued until 1946 or 1947. Then began the Cold War proper, when the West, in Walter Lippmann's words, "came to the conclusion that they must wage a diplomatic campaign to prevent Russia from expanding her sphere, to prevent her from consolidating it, and to compel her to contract it." (In the context of 1947 the last two objectives were no less important than the first.) Whether the West was justified in doing this, as Kennan and others now seem to doubt, need not detain us; the point is that this marked the period of the alliances, when "communism" and "Soviet power" were used as interchangeable terms by both sides. It ended with the Cuban confrontation of 1962. Now, in the fourth stage, each Power seems concerned to prevent the spread of the other's political system only inside its own accepted sphere.

Naturally, during the third stage, when each side was actively concerned with repelling the other, acceptance of such spheres of influence was out of the question. In the view of the West the U.S.S.R. was simply acting on Lenin's advice, "raising revolts against the capitalists, and in the event of necessity coming out even with armed force against the exploiting classes and their states"; while to the Russians the Americans were suppressing genuine revolutionary movements under cover of the Truman Doctrine's reference to armed minorities subjugating a free people. Only since 1962 has there been any real prospect of a new agreement over boundaries. This is the case today. The difference is that the spheres of influence in question extend far beyond the half dozen Balkan states which were tossed about by Churchill and Stalin.

In Europe the boundary runs along the Berlin Wall and the frontier between East and West Germany. In Asia it coincides with the 38th parallel in Korea and the 17th parallel in Vietnam. Within these "zones" Czechoslovakia, Rumania and Cuba fall to the Russians, but Yugoslavia does not.

"Spheres of influence" is perhaps not the best term to use. The states inside are not necessarily subservient to the Power concerned; nor do they all have the same type of government. All that identifies them is that they do not have the political system of the other Power. But there is nothing new in a concept of this kind; and the Monroe Doctrine can usefully be resurrected to define this new relationship between Russia and the United States.

When President Monroe first announced his ban on new European colonies inside the Western hemisphere, he was careful to add to it a ban on Europe's "essentially different" political system; and President Kennedy was equally careful to quote this part of the Doctrine at the time of the confrontation. The sending of Soviet missiles for Castro's use was offensive enough, but so was the presence in Cuba of a communist regime; and Mr. Stevenson's statement, already quoted, is in strict accord with the pronouncement of Monroe. By that time, too, President Eisenhower had refined the Doctrine further. He made it clear that it was not necessary to prove Europe guilty of imposing such a government; in future the Monroe Doctrine would apply whether the government was the result of "invasion, coercion or subversion." By using it to cover American intervention in Guatemala, with which Russia had nothing to do, he had already set a precedent not just for Kennedy in Cuba but for Johnson in the Dominican Republic. (Here Eisenhower brought the Doctrines of Monroe and Truman into line. For the latter had from the first committed America to support governments threatened by "armed minorities" as well as "outside pressures." The difference is that the Truman Doctrine, proclaimed when spheres of influence were not respected, was designed to apply outside the American hemisphere.)

Neither Eisenhower nor Kennedy intended, of course, to revive the Monroe Doctrine as a whole. Had they done so the United States would have been obliged to withdraw from NATO and to recognise East Germany, both of which were out of the question. But the stage was set. Part at least of the Doctrine had been reaffirmed; and the habit of thinking in terms of spheres of influence returned with it. But to apply the Monroe Doctrine today beyond its traditional limits depends upon the Soviet definition of the American sphere of influence. If the Russians are prepared to accept the 17th parallel in Vietnam as part of the boundary, then some of the political difficulties about America's position can be overcome. They are unlikely to accept the concept of two sovereign states in Vietnam, one of which has committed aggression against the other. They are even less likely to accept anything which smacks of the Truman Doctrine; for the whole point of the latter was its universality, a reaction against the concept of spheres of influence unjustly associated with Roosevelt and Stettinius. To secure Russian agreement, or indifference, to American policies in South East Asia, some spheres-of-influence agreement is clearly necessary in principle. It has already begun to exist in practice.

A MONROE DOCTRINE FOR THE RUSSIANS?

There is evidence that the Americans are now thinking along the lines suggested. In an exhaustive survey of foreign policy shortly after his intervention in the Dominican Republic, President Johnson revealed the results of many months of deliberation on the part of both his Defence Secretary, Mr. McNamara, and the chairman of the State Department's policy planning council, Mr. Rostow. As *The Times* Washington Correspondent put it (May 5, 1965) :

More than one sophisticated doctrine has been absorbed, but the basic approach is as follows:
With the nuclear balance established, the status quo can be maintained only by preventing communist wars of liberation from upsetting the ideological balance. Hence the determination to defend the 17th parallel in Vietnam; hence the armed intervention in the Dominican Republic.

At the same time it was made clear that although the American sphere stretched as far as Vietnam, there would be no activist foreign policy:

The Monroe Doctrine is now being universally applied in the East-West dispute . . . to maintain the nuclear, territorial and ideological status quo. The objectives of Monroe and President Johnson are identical.

And with a flash of insight which anticipated the events of three years, the same correspondent added, "It is of course possible that the Soviet Union will see some merit in this super-Power approach that accepts a Hungary as well as a Dominican Republic."
But it was left, not for the first time, for Walter Lippmann to spell out the implications for Czechoslovakia and Vietnam, and possibly for Rumania and Chile.

It is normal, not abnormal, for a Great Power to insist that within its sphere of influence no other Great Power shall exercise hostile military and political force. . . . Great Powers will resist the invasion of their spheres of influence. The Soviet Union did that in Hungary, France did it recently in Gabon, the British have always done it when the Low Countries were attacked, the United States has done it in the Dominican Republic. . . .
The acceptance of spheres of influence has been the diplomatic foundation of the détente in Europe between the Soviet Union and the West. Eventually it will provide the formula of coexistence between Red China and the United States.

Whether the Americans will allow the Russians the same licence in principle as they have now done in practice is more problematical. It is much more probable now than it was before 1962, in the days of the Cold War and the Truman Doctrine. Whether the Russians merely assumed that they could safely take the same kind of action over Czechoslovakia as the Americans did over the Dominican Republic, or whether they had a more substantial understanding, is not known; but they were entitled to recall the words of an American Secretary of State which were spoken the last time there was an understanding over spheres of influence.

We surely cannot and will not deny to other nations the right to develop such a policy [as the Monroe Doctrine]. Far from opposing, we have sympathised with, for example, the effort of the Soviet Union to draw into closer and more friendly association with her Central and East European neighbours. . . . We can appreciate the determination of the people of the Soviet Union that never again will they tolerate the pursuit of policies in these countries deliberately directed against the Soviet Union's security and way of life.[1]

Whether the Russians did recall them or not, the final sentence of Mr. Byrnes's statement, even without the gratuitous addition of the last four words, is quite sufficient to seal the fate of any number of Dubceks; and both the political and military facts suggest that this line of thought is once more being taken up. Which rather implies that the French were not altogether wrong in remonstrating at the time of the invasion of Czechoslovakia that the country had already been sacrificed. Unfortunately, by firing at the wrong target of Yalta, they enabled the argument to be sidestepped.

We are thus led to the conclusion that there are two Powers almost equally prepared to suppress revolutionary change in considerable parts of the earth; and that what is left of the Cold War is only their reluctance to admit it.

[1] James Byrnes, October 31, 1945 (*New York Herald Tribune,* November 1, 1945). Significantly, Mr. Byrnes does not propose consulting Eastern Europe on this point, and makes no mention of any free elections. In this he is strictly in line with the Yalta *Declaration on Liberated Europe,* which, while upholding the principle of free elections, permitted the powers only to "jointly assist . . . where, in their judgment, conditions require"; and even then all three had to be in agreement. The popular view that the Russians were bound by the terms of Yalta to hold free elections inside their sphere is wholly fallacious. The only countries so pledged were the liberated states themselves. See on this Brian Thomas, "Stalin's Blue Pencil," *The Guardian,* August 31, 1968.

selected bibliography

The Cold War has been examined in innumerable books and articles, which of necessity are based only in part on primary sources. The *Department of State Bulletin* provides the texts of official statements and treaties and executive agreements. State Department policy is to make available a full documentary record after a twenty-year interval through the publication of volumes in the *Foreign Relations of the United States* series. In practice, the volumes are presently running about five year behind schedule; the most recently published are those for 1946.

Several works survey American Cold War policy, including: John Spanier, *American Foreign Policy since World War II,* rev. ed. (New York, 1968); William G. Carleton, *The Revolution in American Foreign Policy: Its Global Range* (New York, 1964); David Rees, *The Age of Containment: The Cold War, 1945–1965* (New York, 1967); Norman Graebner, *Cold War Diplomacy: American Foreign Policy, 1945–1960* (Princeton, 1962); Paul Seabury, *The Rise and Decline of the Cold War* (New York, 1967); Paul Y. Hammond, *The Cold War Years: American Foreign Policy since 1945* (New York, 1969); Louis J. Halle, *The Cold War as History* (London, 1967); André Fontaine, *History of the Cold War,* 2 Vols. (New York, 1969); Desmond Donnely, *Struggle for the World: The Cold War, 1917–1965* (New York, 1965); John Lukacs, *A New History of the Cold War,* 3d ed. (Garden City, 1966); Adam B. Ulam, *The Rivals: America and Russia since World War II* (New York, 1971); Stephen E. Ambrose, *Rise to Globalism: American Foreign Policy since 1938* (Baltimore, 1971).

Of the many general critiques of American policy, the following are among the more comprehensive and thoughtful: Ronald Steel, *Pax Americana,* rev. ed. (New York, 1970); Edmund Stillman and William Pfaff, *Power and Impotence* (New York, 1966); J. William Fulbright, *Old Myths and New Realities and Other Commentaries* (New York, 1964), and *The Arrogance of Power* (New York, 1967).

The writings of William A. Williams, most notably *The Tragedy of American Diplomacy,* rev. ed. (New York, 1962), provide a basis for much of the New Left scholarship on foreign policy. Revisionist treatments of the Cold War era include: D. F. Fleming, *The Cold War and Its Origins, 1917–1960,* 2 vols. (New York, 1961), an early and now outdated study; David Horowitz, *The Free World Colossus: A Critique of American Policy in the Cold War,* rev. ed. (New York, 1971), a provocative polemic; Walter LaFeber, *America, Russia, and the Cold War, 1945–1966* (New York, 1967), a careful and balanced treatment. America's role as a "counterrevolutionary" power is important in much revisionist writing, notably: Neal D. Houghton, ed., *Struggle against History: U.S. Foreign Policy in an Age of Revolution* (New York, 1968); Richard J. Barnet, *Intervention and Revolution: The United States in the Third World* (Cleveland, 1968); David Horowitz, ed., *Containment and Revolution* (Boston, 1967).

The revisionist position on the origins of the Cold War is fully presented in the following: Barton J. Bernstein, ed., *Politics and Policies of the Truman Administration* (Chicago, 1970); Lloyd Gardner, *Architects of Illusion: Men and Ideas in American Foreign Policy, 1941–1949* (Chicago, 1970); Gar Alperovitz, *Atomic Diplomacy: Hiroshima and Potsdam, the Use of the Atomic Bomb and the American Confrontation with Soviet Power* (New York, 1965), and *Cold War Essays* (Garden City, 1970); Thomas G. Paterson, "The Abortive American Loan to Russia and the Origins of the Cold War, 1943–1946," *Journal of American History* 56 (June 1969): 93–114; Les K. Adler and Thomas G. Paterson, "Red Fascism: The Merger of Nazi Germany and Soviet Russia in the American Image of Totalitarianism," *American Historical Review* 75 (April 1970): 1046–64; Thomas G. Paterson, ed., *Cold War Critics, Alternatives to American Foreign Policy in the Truman Years* (Chicago, 1971); Thomas G. Paterson, "Eastern Europe and the Early Cold War: The Danube Controversy," *The Historian* 33 (February 1971): 237–47. The most comprehensive revisionist statement on the early Cold War is Joyce and Gabriel Kolko's eight-hundred-page work, *The Limits of Power: The World and United States Foreign Policy, 1945–1954* (New York, 1972). Richard M. Freeland, *The Truman Doctrine and the Origins of McCarthyism: Foreign Policy, Domestic Policy and Internal Security, 1946–1948* (New York, 1972), argues that Truman's militant foreign policy encouraged a domestic anticommunist crusade.

The revisionist position on the origins of the Cold War has drawn some lengthy commentaries and vigorous rebuttals: Paul Seabury, "Cold War Origins," *Journal of Contemporary History* 3 (January 1968): 160–82; "Origins of the Post-War Crisis, A Discussion," ibid. (April 1968): 217–52; John Snell, "The Cold War: Four Contemporary Appraisals," *American Historical Review* 67 (October 1962): 69–75; Norman A. Graebner, "Cold War Origins and the Continuing Debate: A Review of Recent Literature," *Journal of Conflict Resolution* 13 (March 1969): 123–32; Robert W. Sellen, "Origins of the Cold War: An Historiographical Survey," *West Georgia College Studies in the Social Sciences* 9 (June 1970): 57–98; Charles S.

Maier, "Revisionism and the Interpretation of Cold War Origins," *Perspectives in American History* 4 (1970) : 313–47.

Arthur M. Schlesinger, Jr., "Origins of the Cold War," *Foreign Affairs* 66 (October 1967) : 22–52, upholds the traditional interpretation of the origins of the Cold War and criticizes the revisionists. Herbert Feis, *From Trust to Terror: The Onset of the Cold War, 1945–1950* (New York, 1970) restates the substance of the orthodox interpretation and ignores the revisionist scholarship. John Lewis Gaddis, *The United States and the Origins of the Cold War* (New York, 1972) provides a comprehensive and balanced appraisal of American policy. George C. Herring, "Lend-Lease to Russia and the Origins of the Cold War," *Journal of American History* 56 (June 1969) : 93–114, challenges the revisionist contention that the curtailment of Lend-Lease assistance had a political motive. Lawrence S. Kaplan, "The United States and the Origins of NATO, 1946–1949," *Review of Politics* 31 (April 1969) : 210–22, appraises the departure from isolationism.

The issues in central and eastern Europe which brought on the Cold War have been examined in: Martin F. Herz, *Beginnings of the Cold War* (Bloomington, Ind., 1966) ; John L. Snell, *Wartime Origins of the East-West Dilemma over Germany* (New Orleans, 1959) ; Philip E. Mosely, "The Dismemberment of Germany," *Foreign Affairs* 28 (April 1950) : 487–98, and "The Occupation of Germany," ibid. (July 1950) : 580–604; John Gimbel, *The American Occupation of Germany; Politics and the Military* (Stanford, 1968) ; Stephen G. Xydis, *Greece and the Great Powers, 1944–1947: Prelude to the Truman Doctrine* (Salonika, Greece, 1963) ; Stephen G. Xydis, "America, Britain, and the USSR in the Greek Arena, 1944–1947," *Political Science Quarterly* 67 (December 1963) : 581–96; Bruce Kurlick, "The Division of Germany and American Policy on Reparations," *Western Political Quarterly* 23 (June 1970) : 276–93.

Studies of Soviet foreign policy, which help place the Cold War in perspective, include the following general works: Adam B. Ulam, *Expansion and Coexistence: The History of Soviet Foreign Policy, 1917–67* (New York, 1968) ; George F. Kennan, *Russia and the West under Lenin and Stalin* (Boston, 1960) ; Herbert S. Dinerstein, *Fifty Years of Soviet Foreign Policy* (Baltimore, 1968) ; Marshall D. Shulman, *Stalin's Foreign Policy Reappraised* (Cambridge, Mass., 1963) ; Isaac Deutscher, *The Great Contest: Russia and the West* (New York, 1960) ; David J. Dallin, *Soviet Foreign Policy After Stalin* (Philadelphia, 1961) ; Robert C. Tucker, *The Soviet Political Mind* (New York, 1963) ; Zbigniew Brzezinski, *Ideology and Power in Soviet Politics* (New York, 1962) ; Philip E. Mosely, *The Kremlin and World Politics* (New York, 1960). An important comparative study is Zbigniew Brzezinski and Samuel K. Huntington, *Poltical Power: U.S.A.-U.S.S.R.* (New York, 1964).

Several works have examined the arms race and the problem of arms limitations: Bernhard G. Bechhoefer, *Postwar Negotiations for Arms Control* (Washington, D.C., 1961) ; Donald G. Brennan, ed., *Arms Control, Disarmament, and National Security* (New York, 1961) ; Joseph I. Lieberman,

*The Scorpion and the Tarantula: The Struggle to Control Atomic Weapons,
1945–1949* (Boston, 1970); Alexander Dallin, *et al., The Soviet Union and
Disarmament* (New York, 1964); Richard J. Barnet, "The Soviet Attitude on
Disarmament," *Problems of Communism* 10 (May–June 1961): 32–37;
Walter C. Clemens, Jr., "Ideology in Soviet Disarmament Policy," *Journal of
Conflict Resolution* 8 (March 1964): 7–22. The background to the Nuclear
Test Ban Treaty is presented by: Arthur H. Dean, *Test Ban and Disarmament:
The Path of Negotiation* (New York, 1966); Lincoln P. Bloomfield,
Walter C. Clemens, Jr., and Franklyn Griffiths, *Khrushchev and the Arms
Race: Soviet Interests in Arms Control and Disarmament, 1954–1964*
(Cambridge, Mass., 1966); Harold K. Jacobson and Eric Stein, *Diplomats,
Scientists, and Politicians: The United States and the Nuclear Test Ban
Negotiations* (Ann Arbor, Mich., 1966); Carl Kaysen, "Keeping the
Strategic Balance," *Foreign Affairs* 46 (July 1968): 665–75; Robert L.
Rothstein, "Nuclear Proliferation and American Policy," *Political Science
Quarterly* 82 (March 1967): 14–34.

The studies of the origins of the Cold War, of course, focus on the Truman
administration. In addition to the works mentioned previously, other sources
include some important memoirs: Harry S. Truman, *Memoirs,* 2 vols.
(Garden City, N.Y., 1955–56); Dean Acheson, *Present at the Creation*
(New York, 1969); George F. Kennan, *Memoirs, 1925–1950* (Boston, 1967);
James F. Byrnes, *Speaking Frankly* (New York, 1947). Arthur H. Vandenberg,
The Private Papers of Senator Vandenberg (Boston, 1952), and Walter
Millis, ed., *The Forrestal Diaries* (New York, 1951), are also valuable.
Besides the Bernstein book cited previously, the only general survey of the
Truman years is Cabell B. Phillips, *The Truman Presidency: The History of
a Triumphant Succession* (New York, 1966). On the Korean War, the
standard study is John W. Spanier, *The Truman-MacArthur Controversy and
the Korean War* (New York, 1965); the decision to intervene is thoroughly
explored by Glenn D. Paige, *The Korean Decision, June 24–30, 1950*
(New York, 1968); the military and diplomatic positions of the United
States, the Soviet Union, and China are presented by Morton H. Halperin,
"The Limiting Process in the Korean War," *Political Science Quarterly* 78
(March 1963): 13–39; the Chinese intervention is studied by Allen Whiting,
China Crosses the Yalu (New York, 1960).

On the Eisenhower years, the most comprehensive evaluation is John Emmet
Hughes, *The Ordeal of Power* (New York, 1963). Other appraisals include:
Norman Graebner, "Eisenhower's Popular Leadership," *Current History* 39
(October 1960): 230–36, 244; William V. Shannon, "Eisenhower as
President," *Commentary* 26 (November 1958): 390–98; Elmer Plischke,
"Eisenhower's 'Correspondence Diplomacy' with the Kremlin: Case Study in
Summit Diplomatics," *Journal of Politics* 30 (February 1968): 137–59;
Norman Graebner, *The New Isolationism: A Study in Politics and Foreign
Policy since 1950* (New York, 1956). Dwight D. Eisenhower also
wrote fairly candid and revealing memoirs: *The White House Years:
Mandate for Change, 1953–1956* (Garden City, N.Y., 1963), and *The
White House Years: Waging Peace* (Garden City, N.Y., 1965). Secretary